Becoming A

MIGHTY MAN
of God

Ray L. Hawkins, Ph.D.
with
A.B. Gale

xulon
PRESS

Dedication

This book is dedicated to the two mightiest men in my life. Over the years, I have had several good examples and role models in my life. There have been men who acted as youth ministers, coaches, friends of the family and church leaders for me. But only two stand out as truly MIGHTY MEN.

If a MIGHTY MAN is one who is growing spiritually, challenging himself with the lessons God teaches us through His Word and becoming a strong example to others, then my two MIGHTY MEN are my sons, Zach and Eric.

They have taught me more than I have ever taught them. They are spiritually stronger already at their young ages than I ever was at their age. And they are already examples of godly men who want to do what's right…and do it in the right way.

Thanks for being an inspiration for the development of this study series and for being an inspiration for the direction of my life.

Dad

Six Months of Personal Training to Build your
Spiritual, Relational and Emotional Self

Table of Contents

1. Adam	Gen 3:6-9	Hiding Ourselves from God	11
2. Cain	Gen 4:6-7	When Anger Acts Out	17
3. Noah	Gen 6:9	Obedience vs. Logic	23
4. Abraham	Gen 12	You Want Me to go Where?	29
5. Lot	Gen 13:8-11	It's All About Me	35
6. Isaac	Gen 24:66-67	Leaving and Cleaving	39
7. Jacob	Gen 27	Three Steps to Doom	43
8. Esau	Gen 27:38	Oh, a Tough Guy, Eh?	51
9. Onan	Gen 38:8-10	Pleasure without Responsibility	57
10. Joseph	Gen 45:1-8	God Leads my Life	63

11. Moses	Gen 3:11-4:13	But I Can't Do That!	69
12. Pharaoh	Ex. 10:27	Choosing to Have a Hard Heart	75
13. Gideon	Judges 6:36-40	God's Waiting on You	79
14. Jephthah	Judges 11:29-31	Be Careful Making Promises You Can't Keep	87
15. Samson	Judges 16	Evil Companions Corrupt	93
16. Eli	I Sam 2:12	Leading the People, but Losing the Kids	101
17. Samuel	I Sam 3:10	Listening for God	107
18. Saul	I Sam 10:26-27	Knowing When to Keep Your Mouth Shut	113
19. David	II Sam 11	Focus or Blips	117
20. Solomon	I Kings 4:29-30	Head and heart — God wants both	123
21. Azariah	II Chron. 15:1-2	Sticking With God	127
22. Josiah	II Chron. 34:1-2	What are You Worshipping?	131
23. Summary Lesson			139

Introduction

Becoming a MIGHTY MAN of God. It is a notable and perhaps challenging goal for all men in the church today. Why a need for a group of Mighty Men? The church desperately lacks the strong leadership she needs to wage war against the powers of sin and against the effects of a compromising culture. We see times throughout the Bible in which God needed strong men to rise up and start a revolution of change-

-Changing from laid-back watchers to in-the-middle-of-the-battle doers
-Becoming church and family leaders instead of reluctant and whiney followers
-Being transformed from "pew-potatoes" to mighty ministers of evangelism
-Revitalizing our faith and sharing it boldly with others rather than keeping our heads down and our voices quiet.

If there ever was a need for a group of Mighty Men in today's church, certainly the time is now. We need the kind of men who joined David in I Chronicles 12 to turn Saul's Kingdom over to him. Many noteworthy men are mentioned:

Men of Judah, warriors ready for battle.
Famous men of Ephraim.

Experienced soldiers prepared for battle…with undivided loyalty….from Zebulun.

And men of Issachar who understood the times and knew what Israel should do!

We desperately need some modern men of Issachar in our Christian churches today- men who understand the effects of our culture on young people, our families, and our Christian movement and who know what the church should do! For every church that has a group of these type men, surely there are five others that do not. The situation is serious.

It is time to rise up. It is time to "MAN UP!"

Come along with me through this journey as we both become greater Mighty Men for God! Stay with me for 23 weeks…half a year, to make you twice the man for God.

Ray

Adam
Hiding Ourselves from God
Genesis 3:1-7

*1 The serpent was the shrewdest of all the wild animals the L*ORD *God had made. One day he asked the woman, "Did God really say you must not eat the fruit from any of the trees in the garden?"*

2 "Of course we may eat fruit from the trees in the garden," the woman replied. 3 "It's only the fruit from the tree in the middle of the garden that we are not allowed to eat. God said, 'You must not eat it or even touch it; if you do, you will die.'"

4 "You won't die!" the serpent replied to the woman. 5 "God knows that your eyes will be opened as soon as you eat it, and you will be like God, knowing both good and evil."

6 The woman was convinced. She saw that the tree was beautiful and its fruit looked delicious, and she wanted the wisdom it would give her. So she took some of the fruit and ate it. Then she gave some to her husband, who was with her, and he ate it, too. 7 At that moment their eyes were opened, and they suddenly felt shame at their nakedness. So they sewed fig leaves together to cover themselves.

So, imagine this. You wake up one day as an adult instead of a baby, seeing the most beautiful garden around you and a bunch of animals staring at you—-as surprised to see you as you are to see them. Add the fact that you are the only human on the face of the earth, and the first at that! That is the beginning of the story of Adam.

God created Adam and placed him in an incredible garden, giving him the rights and the responsibilities of ownership. Very quickly into his new life, he discovers that he is to care for this place, and that in it is every good thing for food and beauty. It is not long before God realizes that it is not good for Adam to be alone in the garden and creates Eve.

> *And the Lord God said, "It is not good for the man to be alone. I will make a companion who will help him." Gen. 2:18........So the Lord God caused Adam to fall into a deep sleep. He took one of Adam's ribs and closed up the place from which he had taken it. Then the Lord God made a woman from the rib and brought her to Adam. "At last" Adam exclaimed. "She is part of my own flesh and bone! She will be called 'woman' because she was taken out of a man." Gen. 2: 21-23.*

This is a great story of God's love—-that he would create from man the very perfect partner for him. Together, Adam and Eve lived in the Garden of Eden in freedom, peace, and perfect relationship. In this garden, they could work together, play together, love their animals and their surroundings...and in the evenings have a little chat with God about their day. With four rivers inside the garden, there was always plenty of fresh water, beautiful plants, fresh food and gentle breezes. In short, it was a perfect life.

Here comes the problem for today. While Adam worked well with plants and animals, he didn't do so well with the home responsibilities. He may have already lapsed into the mindset of, "I work outside earning a living. Let Eve take care of everything inside the home." Hmmm. Sound familiar? So, in many ways, Adam abdicated his responsibilities for the home to Eve. He withdrew from his relationship with Eve to remain distracted by the events of his part of the garden.

At a time when, as the head of the house, he should have had input into what fruit Eve was bringing home for supper, he was silent.

At a time when he should have known what Eve was doing with her time and who she was spending it with, he was off watching the grass grow — alone.

So, Eve is set up to be a prime target for the low-life lies Satan began to expound.

Maybe Eve was lonely for someone to talk to.

Perhaps she had stopped talking to Adam because he didn't seem to be listening anymore.

For whatever reason, she fell prey to Satan's temptations.

Now let me be very clear here. Eve is completely responsible for her decisions. She alone is responsible and accountable for her choices. While there may have been factors that made her more susceptible to temptation, the choice was still hers and the responsibility still hers. Just as we are responsible for our choices...no matter what the root or situation, both Adam and Eve were responsible for theirs.

Where was Adam?

Why didn't Eve consult with him prior to giving in to Satan's pleas?

And why did he go along with her as soon as she offered the temptation to him?

Why didn't he just say, "no"?

After the sin of listening to Satan and yielding to the temptation he offered, Adam and Eve's eyes were opened. They suddenly became aware that they were naked. They had been naked all along, but never felt shame or discomfort. Now, suddenly, they felt the need to cover themselves...to hide their imperfections, to distract from their insecurities. They used fig leaves to cover their nakedness.

You and I use a lot more sophisticated items...and not just designer suits and fancy clothing. We use things like

-little white lies to close the deal
-denial to distract the wife

-happy faces at church to keep people from asking
-and a hundred more present day "fig leaves."

We hide because we are afraid for people to see us for what we really are. We hide because if God really knew what we were thinking and desiring (He does!), He might not love us or forgive us. We hide from our responsibilities at home because we don't know what to do. And when we try, it's difficult and quite frankly, it might take too much trouble and work to make a good thing happen.

Challenge:
Consider this week how you hide.
How you hide from God...
How you hide from your responsibilities to your wife and your children...
Spend time this week trying to be more vulnerable to God and less willing to hide from Him. Attempt within your marriage, to "man up" to the responsibilities of being the husband.

Discussion Questions

1. Adam was content to let Eve make choices and decisions for both of them as a couple. How often are you content to abdicate your decision-making responsibilities to your wife or others? With what results?

2. How do you set yourself up to sin by whom you choose to listen to?

3. Why do you think Adam did not speak up and remind Eve that she was being disobedient? Think about a time when not speaking up cost you something. If you feel comfortable, share it with the group.

4. What do you feel shame over?

5. What have you done or what things have you used to cover your shame? How did that work?

6. What has caused you to hide from God? What mechanism of hiding have you tried to use? How has that worked for you?

When Anger Acts Out
Genesis 4:3-8

3 When it was time for the harvest, Cain presented some of his crops as a gift to the LORD. 4 Abel also brought a gift — the best of the firstborn lambs from his flock. The LORD accepted Abel and his gift, 5 but he did not accept Cain and his gift. This made Cain very angry, and he looked dejected.

6 "Why are you so angry?" the LORD asked Cain. "Why do you look so dejected? 7 You will be accepted if you do what is right. But if you refuse to do what is right, then watch out! Sin is crouching at the door, eager to control you. But you must subdue it and be its master."

8 One day Cain suggested to his brother, "Let's go out into the fields."[a] And while they were in the field, Cain attacked his brother, Abel, and killed him.

After Adam and Eve had been kicked out of the Garden of Eden for their sin, they began to do what most families do. They worked for a living, had a few arguments about whose fault it really was that they got kicked out of the Garden, and they had children. Cain and Abel were their names. Remember that at this point, as far as we know, these were the first two people actually born and raised from children into adults. Adam and Eve were created full grown. The first job at parenting was not necessarily done by the best parents. Whether they had ever even heard of their parents' disobedience in the Garden or not, we do not know.

Abel becomes the young man who appears to have the character of conforming to God's offering criteria, while Cain does not. You see, at this point in the Bible, people offered sacrifices as a sign of honoring God and revealing the level of their relationship to Him. Cain becomes a farmer and offers a gift of produce at harvest-time while Abel offers a choice lamb from his flock. God was pleased with Abel's sacrifice, but flatly refused Cain's.

Here's where it gets interesting. Cain becomes really angry. God asks him why he is so angry. Rather than discuss his anger with God and resolve the underlying issues, Cain asks his brother to go out into the fields and there he kills him. There you have it...the first murder in history...over a plate of vegetables! Or better yet, jealousy.

When God asks Cain about his severe anger, he offers some solutions for Cain and a warning.

> *You will be accepted if you do what is right. But if you refuse to do what is right, then watch out! Sin is crouching at the door, eager to control you. But you must subdue it and be its master." vs.7.*

Though Cain never answers God as to the cause of his anger, God tells him that if he will just respond in the right way, he will be accepted. This principle is important for all of us to know. Even after a mistake, God just wants us to do what's right (we call it repent and straighten up). There are hundreds of stories throughout the Bible that teach this principle.

Now, perhaps, Cain's offering was the wrong content. He offered food and although there would be future grain and drink offerings, most future offerings and sacrifices would be animal. To this point in the Bible however, there is no record of God commanding animal sacrifices. If it isn't the content of the sacrifice, perhaps it's Cain's heart. The verse above seems to indicate this and certainly Cain's action immediately after being rejected would suggest a little heart problem! In addition, Hebrews 11:4 states that Abel's sacrifice was offered with more faith than Cain's.

4 It was by faith that Abel brought a more acceptable offering to God than Cain did. Abel's offering gave evidence that he was a righteous man, and God showed his approval of his gifts. Although Abel is long dead, he still speaks to us by his example of faith.

Now is when it hits home with you and me. God tells Cain that if he refuses to respond correctly—-most likely with a good heart attitude—-then Satan will attack and destroy him. What we see here is that Cain's heart attitude was one of anger. And that unloving heart caused him not only to be unhappy with God, but to also be completely open for Satan to rush right in and make himself at home. As soon as this happened, we see the anger turn into hatred, and the hatred turn into murder.

It doesn't take very long for anger to take some negative form. That's when we get into trouble...because anger generally acts out!

We might not murder someone, but think about these common reactions to internalized anger:

—driving like a maniac

—yelling at the kids

—putting a hole in the wall

—withdrawing (passive aggressive anger)

—others

Anger truly is a risky way to feel. In itself, being mad at something is no big deal. If it could just stay there.... or be worked out in the beginning....or held in check before it goes wild. How do you do with your anger? Think back on the last couple of times you have gotten angry.

—Maybe it was with the wife?

—Or with the job?

—Or the game?

—Or the weather?

—Or maybe it was even with God?

How we handle anger and who gets hurt by it are questions we need to consider. It won't get better on its own. Get an accountability partner, hold yourself accountable, learn how to communicate your feelings better, problem solve your issues with others more effectively. Count to 10 if you need to. Do something!

Cain realized toward the end of the story that his punishment for murder included being banished from God's presence. He settled in an area east of Eden which puts him in modern-day Iran. Lasting effects of his anger seem to exist in the inhabitants of that land even today.

Challenge:
This week do something about your anger. Make one positive step toward doing something—anything—about your anger.

Discussion Questions

1. On a scale of 1-10, 1 being passive and 10 being extremely angry, rank your anger response in the following situations:
   —Driving home in traffic after a bad day at work.
   —You find out that your co-worker got the promotion you were expecting to get
   —The wife puts her foot down about your going on her family's vacation trip.

Fill in the top three examples of situations that really stir up your anger below:

2. Name and discuss one bad situation you have been in because of your anger and what you could have done differently. How might you handle this situation better next time?

3. What feelings do you have the most difficulty expressing...and therefore, just act angry instead? (Examples: Disappointment in not being able to have sex with your wife, but act angry instead. Fear that the boss will fire you when he finds out the monthly numbers, but you take the offensive and start griping in anger about him behind his back.)

List the emotions or feelings you have the most difficulty sharing.

4. What would be the advantage for you to have an account-ability partner on anger?

Noah—Build a Boat? Uh—What's a Boat?
Obedience vs. Logic
Genesis 6-7

6 So the LORD was sorry he had ever made them and put them on the earth. It broke his heart. Gen. 6:6.

4 Seven days from now I will make the rains pour down on the earth. And it will rain for forty days and forty nights, until I have wiped from the earth all the living things I have created." Gen. 7:4.

13 That very day Noah had gone into the boat with his wife and his sons—Shem, Ham, and Japheth—and their wives. Gen. 7:13.

On the first day of the new year, ten and a half months after the flood began,¹ the floodwaters had almost dried up from the earth. Noah lifted back the covering of the boat and saw that the surface of the ground was drying. 14 Two more months went by, and at last the earth was dry! Gen. 8:14.

Okay. Here's the problem of the day—-the dilemma du jour. God has just asked you to do something, and it seems a little strange. But you love God, are committed to serving Him, and you really want to be obedient. However, you're not even sure you know how to do what He's asking of you, and it is rather a strange request! Furthermore, you can really see no reason whatsoever for doing this...and did I mention that this is a really strange request?

Would you do it? Or does your answer depend on what He's asking of you? Or does it depend on your level of faith? Or whether it makes sense to you? Or if you really even want to do it? Sometimes what God requires of us seems foolish at the time because we don't have all the pieces of the puzzle, all the yarns in the fabric that God is weaving together in our lives or in the lives of others. But He does. The question is whether or not we trust Him enough to be obedient even when we can't see good reasoning behind the request.

So what is so strange about God's job for Noah? All God did was ask Noah to prepare for a big rain—-what's so unusual about that?

What's so unusual is that prior to this section of Scripture, there is no mention of rain ever occurring. In fact, Hebrews 11:7 says that God warned Noah about something that had never happened before. And that makes the story of Noah and his faith all the more important.

7 It was by faith that Noah built a large boat to save his family from the flood. He obeyed God, who warned him about things that had never happened before. By his faith Noah condemned the rest of the world, and he received the righteousness that comes by faith. Heb. 11:7.

Noah, his wife, his three sons, and their wives were the only souls that weren't evil at that time. Gen 6:6 says that the people had become so evil that God's heart was broken and He was sorry that He had ever made them. So God told Noah to build a boat. Not just any boat...but a really BIG boat.

For people who had never experienced rain, nor seen the need for a boat, this must have been a really strange sight. This is an example of truly living by faith to build such a major project when there seemed no need for it...There must have been ridicule and insults at Noah and his family as they labored day after day to build this boat. They must have gotten tired beyond belief of continually working on this project that seemed never to end. Some commentators believe that it took 120 years to build the boat. If so, Noah and his sons must have wondered when God was going to bring the promised flood. Surely they must have wondered if they were spending all this time and effort being foolish rather than being faithful... And the world certainly saw their task as foolish, but Noah and his family continued being faithful...

It's important to understand that being obedient may not seem to make sense at the time. Never having had rain or floods made this task of boat-building seem irrelevant, un-necessary, and foolish. But God had the big picture and knew that what He was asking Noah to do included the provision for his salvation and that of all creation. Noah had to take God at His word and trust His care by being obedient in faith.

Noah and his family built the boat to God's specifications. When it was finished, God gave Noah one week to gather all the animals according to His directions. Then, when all the animals were inside, Noah and his family entered the boat and that very day, the rain started. God shut them in and sealed the boat.

Then everyone knew that God is true to His word, and being obedient may not seem to make sense, but it always does. Unfortunately, while most of the people came to understand that God is truth personified, it might have been their third time under the water. Like some of us, it might take a few times to get our attention, and even a third or fourth time to get our obedience. It was too late for the people of Noah's day to change their minds or their destiny. It's not too late for you and me!

Only Noah and his family were allowed into the boat that was more like a zoo than a vacation, and were saved from the flood waters. Sometimes God allows second chances, but sometimes the next second chance is the last chance. Sometimes we get into the habit of always counting on next future chances, and eventually they will stop coming. If there's something that you need to change in your life, don't wait for the next second chance. It may not come.

After rain that lasted 40 days and nights, the earth remained covered with water for almost a year. The boat then came to rest on top of Mt. Ararat. After being in the boat all this time, Noah sent out a bird that returned, followed sometime later by a bird that returned with a leaf in its mouth. Sometime later, he sent out a third bird that did not return. Noah knew then, that this bird had found a resting place and that the time had come to leave the boat. They were the only ones who had survived the flood.

Now back to the daily dilemma. Noah endured frustration, ridicule, loss of friends, etc. in order to be faithful to what God had told him to do. Are you willing to be obedient to the same extent?

Were you blessed by your choice? Noah and his entire family were blessed by his.

Challenge:
This week, look for ways to be obedient to God's leading—even when it might not make sense to you.

Discussion Questions

1. Have you ever been called upon to do something for God that didn't seem to make sense at the time? (Think in terms of job moves, family choices, serving others or becoming involved in a church work.)

2. How did this event work out for you? And what did you learn from it?

3. How difficult is it in your life to be obedient to God? In what areas of your life do you most often struggle with doing what's right even if it doesn't make sense to you at the time?

4. Have you ever been ridiculed for doing something right?

5. Have you ever ridiculed someone else for doing something right for God?

6. How might mighty men of God stand up under the pressure of obedience despite the criticisms within and the ridicule outside?

Abraham
You Want me to Go Where?
Genesis 12

1 The Lord had said to Abram, "Leave your native country, your relatives, and your father's family, and go to the land that I will show you. 2 I will make you into a great nation. I will bless you and make you famous, and you will be a blessing to others. 3 I will bless those who bless you and curse those who treat you with contempt. All the families on earth will be blessed through you."

4 So Abram departed as the Lord had instructed, and Lot went with him. Abram was seventy-five years old when he left Haran. 5 He took his wife, Sarai, his nephew Lot, and all his wealth—his livestock and all the people he had taken into his household at Haran—and headed for the land of Canaan.

8b There he built another altar and dedicated it to the Lord, and he worshiped the Lord.

Hebrews 11:8
8 It was by faith that Abraham obeyed when God called him to leave home and go to another land that God would give him as his inheritance. He went without knowing where he was going.

L ast week, we studied the faith of Noah, who God asked to do something and he did it without really questioning. I hope you made a note of some way you obeyed God and stood up for Him, despite the logic inside yourself or the ridicule from others around you. Take a moment to share your experience with those around you.

Let's build on that thought today.

It's difficult enough to move all your belongings, uproot your family members, leave a job, get new cable put in, and move to a new environment these days. It was equally overwhelming (except for the cable part) during the days of Abram. One morning, after Abram had gotten up and started settling into the day, God told him to pick up his belongings and move- no discussing with the wife (Sarai) and no information given regarding a destination. No info about whether there would be water or food available and no ideas as to how far away they were going to travel. And Abram did it!

He trusted God to lead him to fresh water and a food supply. He trusted God for protection from warring tribes along the way. It wasn't a safe thing to travel in those days. In fact, it was a little frightening. And you think that high gas prices are scary!

Abram was 75 years old when he took off on this journey. He took his wife, his nephew Lot and all his wealth and workers. They traveled for a great distance to the unheard of-at least at this time in the Bible- land of Canaan.

Why did Abram do it? Would you?

We are told in the text above that when God called Abram to move, He had already promised him that he would become the father of a great nation. He would be blessed and be a blessing to others. In fact, God told Abram that He would bless those who bless him and curse those who curse him...not a bad assurance to have in a new place! This must have also sounded good to Abram who was 75 and had no children! (The additional part of the promise to Abram was that all people in the world would be blessed through him. We know that God was talking about Christ coming through the lineage of Abram. But Abram didn't understand that!!)

The important point is that God called Abram to move and he moved. God told him to go and he went. God said He'd show him where and Abram trusted God to keep His word. (Hebrews 11:8)

When you are trying to make a decision about a new job or a new house or a new school for the kids, do you pray for God to lead you? In many ways, God speaks to us today.

1. Open doors of opportunity- Sometimes God provides things for us that we have not even thought of before. He might give us a chance to live out the dream we always wanted to live or give us a new dream. One approach to use in following God's lead, is the "Walk through an open door and wait for the next door to open" approach. This simply means that we accept God's gift of opportunity, but wait for God to prove this is Him talking by opening up the next opportunity. Staying in prayer with Him will reveal to you if you should continue taking the next step toward a job, personal commitment or change.

2. Other people- Many times the way God can most speak to us is through trusted companions. Friends, family members and wise Christians can help determine God's will for our decisions because they are on the outside looking in. Although God's ways are not always logical (learned last week from Noah), many times they are easier to see without our own opinions and prejudices. Wise counsel is a great way to a closer relationship with God.

3. Extraordinary things- Making great things happen is no big deal to God, and sometimes He wants to get our attention. When something special happens in your life, question whether God is trying to get your attention and see where He might be asking you to go.

4. Study of the Bible- Whether you are studying a specific section of scripture or just reading whatever you open up to, God's Word may have exactly what you need at any given point in your life.

5. Feeling of confidence- Many question this one, but many times people feel a sense of calm and peace when praying for

a decision and getting one. This is risky in the sense that you have to be careful it is not your own desire coming through. Honest evaluation of listening to God's answers through quiet meditation is a discipline you might want to develop.

This week, try to listen to God's leading and follow through with it.

Challenge:
When Abram arrived at his destination, he built an altar and worshipped God. When we move, what is our focus on? Wonder what it would be like to move because of God, trust Him to provide for us, and worship Him whenever we get there? Think about it.

Discussion Questions:

1. Have you ever seen the hand of God in a decision you made?
   a. After the fact?
   b. While it was working out for you?
   c. Before you even started?

2. When was the last time you think God told you to go somewhere or to do something, and you just trusted Him to take care of the details?

3. What about your personality prevents you from just trusting God's lead?
   a. Control issues
   b. Lack of personal experience in seeing God follow through in your life
   c. Fear of failure (or something else)
   d. Other?

4. Which of the ways God speaks to us today listed previously make sense to you? Which have you used? Which one would you be willing to try this week?

Lot
It's All About Me
Gen. 13:7-11

✠

7 So disputes broke out between the herdsmen of Abram and Lot. (At that time Canaanites and Perizzites were also living in the land.)

8 Finally Abram said to Lot, "Let's not allow this conflict to come between us or our herdsmen. After all, we are close relatives! 9 The whole countryside is open to you. Take your choice of any section of the land you want, and we will separate. If you want the land to the left, then I'll take the land on the right. If you prefer the land on the right, then I'll go to the left."

10 Lot took a long look at the fertile plains of the Jordan Valley in the direction of Zoar. The whole area was well watered everywhere, like the garden of the LORD or the beautiful land of Egypt. (This was before the LORD destroyed Sodom and Gomorrah.) 11 Lot chose for himself the whole Jordan Valley to the east of them. He went there with his flocks and servants and parted company with his uncle Abram.

You remember that thing your mom used to make you do if you had a sister or a brother? There's one piece of pie left and you want to trick your young brother by saying you will cut it in "half" and give him his half. You intend to take the bigger half and hold the pie pan just so…he can't see the difference and you have won. Mom steps in and says, "Good idea, Ray. You cut and your brother will choose." Man, I hated it when Mom interfered in my fair play! We'll get back to this example in a minute…

Lot was Abraham's nephew. He had traveled with his uncle from Ur and Haran after last week's lesson, seeing Abram listen to God's voice and trusting in it. Lot's father had died, and Abram had been like a father substitute ever since. Lot had inherited herds and wealth from his father, and being around Abram, a man of God who was being blessed by God, is not a bad business relationship! He had managed his herds like Abram did and he was being blessed like Abram was being blessed. One day, there arose a problem.

Since both of these men had herds that were growing quite large, the land could not support grazing required for both. Conflict broke out between Abram's and Lot's herdsmen. It appears that other native people were living on the same land and Abram became aware that the behavior of their herdsmen was a bad example of God's people. Being a man of God, Abram decided to solve this example problem. He approached Lot with an offer of conflict resolution. Now, approaching family members with a potential conflict for conflict resolution can be quite conflictual. You know what I mean? If you have ever worked in a family business and tried to fix something, you might have some ideas worth sharing here!

Abram told Lot that he could have his choice of the land and that they would part company. Remember the example from Mom above. Well, here it is in action. Look, Abram knew it was because of him that God was blessing Lot, but he was not being stingy with the wealth or the blessings. He was willing to cut the last piece of pie and let the other person choose the piece.

Lot was not so willing to share. Having always lived in wealth of some degree, he seems to have a sense of entitlement. He exhibits that in his choice.

While Abram was the oldest and the father-figure, he should have had the first choice of the land, but in an act of humility and generosity, he sets an example for Lot by allowing him to have the choice. Lot is so self-centered, he fails to see the example and proceeds to make his selfish choice. Lot pitches his tent toward Sodom, where the grass was green and well watered, and the people were exceedingly wicked. And yes, that is where the word sodomy came from! Wicked indeed! Future stories about Lot illustrate how being surrounded by evil corrupts our own lives as well. But that is for another lesson...

Let's concentrate on Lot's sense of entitlement versus Abram's sense of humility. Today we live in a culture and a country that suggests that we are "entitled" to whatever we can get. If you work hard, climb the corporate ladder and keep your nose to the grindstone (what is a grindstone anyway?), you will get what you deserve. When we do get things- rewards, benefits, money, etc. we have a hard time giving to others in need because they should have worked like we worked.

If the verse is true, "Every good and perfect gift comes from the Father," (James 1:17) then we are mere stewards of what God has given to us. If God has given something to us, it is not necessarily because we have earned it. Blessings are not always earned. If God has given us something, he might be giving us things to share with others in need. Think back at examples in your life of people who gave you...

A chance
A job
A buck
A word of encouragement.

It may have cost them something and it may not have, but still it helped you along your way. Consider the times you have cut the piece of pie and chosen the bigger half. Wonder why God chooses not to treat us this way?

Challenge:
This week try to be the bigger man and take the smaller piece. Feel proud because you have done the right thing, not because you leave with more than someone else.

Discussion Questions

1. Remember the names and situations in which people in your past gave you a "bigger half of the last piece of pie." (Ex. A mom who did without so that you could go to camp, a boss who could have hired a person cheaper but who wanted to help you and your family, or a friend who gave you the benefit of the doubt and stood by you through a tough time.)

2. Be honest now. In what areas do you struggle with your own sense of selfishness or entitlement? Be specific and consider the following areas of your life:
   a. Your marriage
   b. Your children/family
   c. The job
   d. Decisions (whether at home or with friends)
   e. Other

3. Try to remember a time when you took the bigger half of the pie. Why do you think you did that? What were you afraid of? What do you think you deserved? Share this with someone in the group.

Isaac
Leaving and Cleaving
Genesis 24: 66-67

66 Then the servant told Isaac everything he had done.

67 And Isaac brought Rebekah into his mother Sarah's tent, and she became his wife. He loved her deeply, and she was a special comfort to him after the death of his mother.

This is the story about a "mama's boy." Now, not the kind of mama's boy that means in any way he was not very masculine, but rather in the way that he definitely never quite let go of her, even after her death. Let me explain.

The story actually begins long before there is an Isaac...just a promise of him. Abraham was God's chosen person. In fact, God promised Abram and his wife MANY children, as many as the sands of the seashore. We realize now that God was promising him a nation of people, the Israelites, not a "nationful" of children. Abram and Sarai were getting way too old to have many children, and for that matter maybe even one! But finally, God caused Sarai to become pregnant, and they had a son named Isaac. Finally, Sarai had her child...the child of her old age. She must have clung to him tightly so as not to lose him. And then there is that teenage story...

Isaac is also the son that Sarai nearly lost to her own husband nearly killing him. God was testing Abraham's faith by asking him to sacrifice his son...his only son. Sound familiar? Yep, this is one of those "foreshadowing events" in the Old Testament. It is a story that doesn't really make sense to us until we see the story happen again later in the Bible. Obviously, this was a test of Abraham's faith. It was also the story of God sending His son....His only son to actually be sacrificed for human kind. You see, God stopped Abraham from killing his own son at the last minute. He did not do the same for His own Son, Jesus. But for whatever this story means for us today, for Sarai, it must have been a horrific event.

No wonder she may have kept the apron strings tied a little too tightly around her son.

For whatever reasons, those above or others we are not told from the Old Testament, Isaac is also very close to his mother—-so close that when his mother dies, his father tries to find a wife for him. When he succeeds in finding him Rebekah, one of the oddest statements in the Old Testament is made.

Isaac takes Rebekah into the tent of his mother and there he felt comforted at the death of his mother. Ok, come on. By any way you read that, it's a little strange, right?

Why did Abraham not comfort his own son in the death of Sarai? A death they both shared in grieving?

Why did Isaac not have his own tent and not use his mother's tent?

How might have Rebekah felt with the memory of a mother in law she would never be able to meet having such a presence in their marriage?

It is difficult for newlyweds to become adjusted to each other without an 11x14 framed glossy of the mother in law on the nightstand next to the bed! It must have been difficult for Rebekah. This might explain some of the reason why she later had her favorite son and had no hesitation in tricking her husband into blessing her favorite son (Jacob) instead of her husband's favorite (Esau). See that story to review this point.

For our benefit today, let's consider men today who compare their wives to their Mothers. If you've ever done it, be it about cooking or anything else, you have learned it might just cause some conflict! If you've ever called your mom about a decision before you talked to your wife about it, you may have sensed the jealousy and hurt.

Bottom line: This may very well be why *Genesis 2:24* says, *"For this cause shall a man leave his father and mother and cleave to his wife."* Men, there may not be enough "cleavage" in your marriage because there isn't enough "leavage." It is difficult to break away from parents for both good and bad reasons. Unity in your marriage may mean you have to come to terms in several areas of your family of origin, because the family you are responsible for now is the one you have created with your wife.

Ask yourself in what ways you have refused to leave your own parents and have in turn hurt your wife.

Maybe it's in good ways that you want your wife to repeat.

Maybe it's in unresolved resentment you still hold for a parent who did not meet your needs.

It could be a refusal to grow up and assume responsibility for being the man of the house now.

Challenge:
This week look for ways in which you and your wife might work on the "leaving and cleaving" issue together.

Discussion Questions

1. Think of one guy you know (it might be yourself) who is still tied to his mama's apron strings. What do you think about this? How does it seem to make his wife feel?

2. In what ways have you failed to leave your family of origin (mother or father)?

3. Does your wife struggle with this issue more than you do? In what way(s) and how does it make you feel?

4. Have you ever felt that parents (yours or your wife's) have been brought into your marriage- decisions, discussions, vacations, etc- when it bothered you? How might you want to handle that situation differently next time?

5. Name 3 ways in which your marriage could be improved if you and/or your wife worked on leaving and cleaving:
   a.
   b.
   c.

Jacob
Three Steps to Doom
Genesis 27

1 One day when Isaac was old and turning blind, he called for Esau, his older son, and said, "My son." "Yes, Father?" Esau replied.

2 "I am an old man now," Isaac said, "and I don't know when I may die. 3 Take your bow and a quiver full of arrows, and go out into the open country to hunt some wild game for me. 4 Prepare my favorite dish, and bring it here for me to eat. Then I will pronounce the blessing that belongs to you, my firstborn son, before I die."

5 But Rebekah overheard what Isaac had said to his son Esau. So when Esau left to hunt for the wild game, 6 she said to her son Jacob, "Listen. I overheard your father say to Esau, 7 'Bring me some wild game and prepare me a delicious meal. Then I will bless you in the LORD's presence before I die.' 8 Now, my son, listen to me. Do exactly as I tell you. 9 Go out to the flocks, and bring me two fine young goats. I'll use them to prepare your father's favorite dish. 10 Then take the food to your father so he can eat it and bless you before he dies."

11 "But look," Jacob replied to Rebekah, "my brother, Esau, is a hairy man, and my skin is smooth. 12 What if my father touches me? He'll see that I'm trying to trick him, and then he'll curse me instead of blessing me."

13 But his mother replied, "Then let the curse fall on me, my son! Just do what I tell you. Go out and get the goats for me!"

14 So Jacob went out and got the young goats for his mother. Rebekah took them and prepared a delicious meal, just the way Isaac liked it. 15 Then she took Esau's favorite clothes, which were there in the house, and gave them to her younger son, Jacob. 16 She covered his arms and the smooth part of his neck with the skin of the young goats. 17 Then she gave Jacob the delicious meal, including freshly baked bread.

18 So Jacob took the food to his father. "My father?" he said. "Yes, my son," Isaac answered. "Who are you—Esau or Jacob?"

19 Jacob replied, "It's Esau, your firstborn son. I've done as you told me. Here is the wild game. Now sit up and eat it so you can give me your blessing."

*20 Isaac asked, "How did you find it so quickly, my son?" "The L*ORD *your God put it in my path!" Jacob replied.*

21 Then Isaac said to Jacob, "Come closer so I can touch you and make sure that you really are Esau." 22 So Jacob went closer to his father, and Isaac touched him. "The voice is Jacob's, but the hands are Esau's," Isaac said. 23 But he did not recognize Jacob, because Jacob's hands felt hairy just like Esau's. So Isaac prepared to bless Jacob. 24 "But are you really my son Esau?" he asked. "Yes, I am," Jacob replied.

25 Then Isaac said, "Now, my son, bring me the wild game. Let me eat it, and then I will give you my blessing." So Jacob took the food to his father, and Isaac ate it. He also drank the wine that Jacob served him. Then Isaac said to Jacob, 26 "Please come a little closer and kiss me, my son."

27 So Jacob went over and kissed him. And when Isaac caught the smell of his clothes, he was finally convinced, and he blessed his son. He said, "Ah! The smell of my son is like the smell of the outdoors, which the LORD has blessed!

*28 "From the dew of heaven
and the richness of the earth,
may God always give you abundant harvests of grain
and bountiful new wine.*

*29 May many nations become your servants,
and may they bow down to you.
May you be the master over your brothers,
and may your mother's sons bow down to you.
All who curse you will be cursed,
and all who bless you will be blessed."*

30 As soon as Isaac had finished blessing Jacob, and almost before Jacob had left his father, Esau returned from his hunt. 31 Esau prepared a delicious meal and brought it to his father. Then he said, "Sit up, my father, and eat my wild game so you can give me your blessing."

32 But Isaac asked him, "Who are you?" Esau replied, "It's your son, your firstborn son, Esau."

33 Isaac began to tremble uncontrollably and said, "Then who just served me wild game? I have already eaten it, and I blessed him just before you came. And yes, that blessing must stand!"

34 When Esau heard his father's words, he let out a loud and bitter cry. "Oh my father, what about me? Bless me, too!" he begged.

35 But Isaac said, "Your brother was here, and he tricked me. He has taken away your blessing."

36 Esau exclaimed, "No wonder his name is Jacob, for now he has cheated me twice, First he took my rights as the firstborn, and now he has stolen my blessing. Oh, haven't you saved even one blessing for me?"

37 Isaac said to Esau, "I have made Jacob your master and have declared that all his brothers will be his servants. I have guaranteed him an abundance of grain and wine — what is left for me to give you, my son?"

38 Esau pleaded, "But do you have only one blessing? Oh my father, bless me, too!" Then Esau broke down and wept.

39 Finally, his father, Isaac, said to him,
"You will live away from the richness of the earth,
and away from the dew of the heaven above.

40 You will live by your sword,
and you will serve your brother.
But when you decide to break free,
you will shake his yoke from your neck."

41 From that time on, Esau hated Jacob because their father had given Jacob the blessing. And Esau began to scheme: "I will soon be mourning my father's death. Then I will kill my brother, Jacob."

Jacob was the second-born twin of Isaac and Rebekah, you remember—the one who stole his brother's birthright and later his blessing. We studied Esau, the brother who gave the first one away and lost the second one by deception. Today we look at the story from Jacob's perspective.

As you recall, father Isaac was so old he could barely see and could probably hear even less. He told his favorite son Esau to go and hunt wild game and fix him some stew the way he liked it…and probably the way his wife Rebekah wouldn't fix it for him! Guys, know the feeling? Isaac's plan was to bless his son Esau, but Rebekah was going to have none of that!

Well, anyway, notice Jacob's **Three Steps to Doom:**

Step One- Devising the Scheme

When his mother overheard the above plot, she devised a scheme to trick the old man into blessing her favorite son instead of his father's favorite. She fixed the stew and put animal hair on Jacob's arms to make him look like his brother. Even though Jacob appears to have some issue with this scheme at the very beginning, he goes along with it. After all, his mom was telling him to do it. After all, he really was the better son and deserved the inheritance. After all… after all…after all… It seems easy to rationalize plans when they make so much sense in our own heads doesn't it? Many times we, just like Jacob, can easily justify a scheme to get back at someone, or a plan to beat someone to the punch, or to take credit for something we really didn't do. After all, it really should have been us. The other guy didn't deserve the break. We've worked harder, been here longer, and are better in our own minds.

It's not that we always come up with the plan ourselves. Just like Jacob, someone else often tells us something to do, a way they have beat the system or got a return on the taxes. Surely we aren't as guilty if we don't come up with the plan ourselves.

And just like Jacob, sometimes the person suggesting it is someone important in our lives. For him it was his mother. For us, it might be a boss, or a coach, or the entire team or just society at large. We don't often need too much influence to do something wrong, but there are times when standing up for the right might mean losing face in front of significant others. You think that peer pressure is just for kids?

Step Two-Putting It into Motion

Most often, this part of the process includes the 3 deadly sins of men- **LYING, STEALING AND CHEATING.**
Lying- Lying is both the blatant saying of something that is not true for the express purpose of trying to deceive someone, as well as the remaining quiet and allowing someone to assume something that is equally wrong. Most of us lie well because we start doing it so early in life. Very young children can tell little "white lies" and learn the process of getting away with things. By the time we are teens, we become pretty adept at it, especially with our parents, friends and our teachers. If we work really hard at perfecting this negative trait, we use it for the rest of our lives through our business world, in our personal relationships, and with everyone we meet.

I am not sure how good at lying Jacob was, but he had to do it right to his father's face several times during this conversation. His father questions his identity on at least 4 times throughout the encounter before blessing him. I wonder if Jacob found that it really is easier to lie the 2nd, 3rd, and 15th time?

Stealing- Stealing doesn't have to be as blatant as Jacob's was in the story above. He took away his brother's inheritance and left him with nothing. We often times steal little things (office supplies from work) or parts of people (manipulating a boss to believe something that is not true about a co-worker, and therefore trusting you because you told him what he thinks is true) or someone's future (by not telling them about the salvation available to them in Jesus 'cause we don't want to be bothered.)

Stealing comes in many different forms, but taking anything that rightfully belongs to someone else- a thing or a word of encourage-ment, a promotion or a belief system- and keeping it for yourself is stealing.

Cheating- You have cheated if you end up with anything that you have not rightfully worked for or received. We call it cheating on a test when you **STEAL** the answers from a friend's paper and **LIE** to your teacher about whether you answered the questions yourself. In many ways, cheating becomes the culmination of both of the first two. There is little you can cheat on without the help of your evil twin brothers- Lying and Stealing.

Step Three- **Running from it**

Jacob cheated his brother Esau out of both his birthright and his inheritance by lying and stealing. You might want to know about something that later happens to Jacob.. Remember that when Jacob falls in love with Rachel, a beautiful young woman and agrees to work for her for seven years, Laban deceives him and tricks him into marrying the ugly sister Leah and working additional years for Rachel. Hmmm. There always seems to be someone better at the game than we are. To avoid being hurt and taken advantage of, don't play the deception game at all. If you start it, someone else will probably finish it. My mother used to tell me, "What goes around, comes around." Well, the truth is that some times in life you will be able to get away with things. But eventually, it comes back to bite you.

Running from our mistakes creates a greater chance for this to happen. Face the music, address the mistake, accept responsibility for it. Who knows what negative things Jacob could have avoided if he had not let this event of "Doom" go unaddressed. We all would be better off to take the punishment, learn from it, and move on.

Challenge:
Focus on being responsible for your own actions this week.... rather than lying, cheating, or stealing, to get out of the circumstances that you're in.

Discussion Questions:

1. In reviewing the three steps to Doom, think of a time in which you have devised a scheme, put it into motion by lying, stealing and cheating, and then run from it. You may not feel comfortable sharing this with others in your group, but share with them the one part of the 3 step process that you do easiest.

2. Share an example of your own or someone else you know, who had the "What goes around, comes around" philosophy hit home and come true.

3. Most men "run" because it is easier to try to keep the lie going than to confront it. What are some ways men have to pay prices for confronting the truth?
   a. In business
   b. In guy friendships
   c. With your wife
   d. With the kids
   e. At church

4. Try to share one way you will teach your children, if you have them, about this 3 step process. How will you get them to listen to you and believe it?

Esau
Oh, a Tough Guy, Eh?
Genesis 27:37-38

37 Isaac said to Esau, "I have made Jacob your master and have declared that all his brothers will be his servants. I have guaranteed him an abundance of grain and wine—what is left for me to give you, my son?"

38 Esau pleaded, "But do you have only one blessing? Oh my father, bless me, too!" Then Esau broke down and wept.

Esau was a tough guy—-you know a man's man. He was capable of living in the elements, fending for himself, hunting for wild animals, and handling anything else nature could dish out. Yep, he was strong and tough. He had muscles where most of us never thought we could develop them...of course dragging dead animals from the woods back home can build up a few muscles! I imagine that Esau knew when the best time to fish was, where the best hiding places for wild game were...and he always had a quiver full of sharpened arrows on one shoulder and a bow stretched across his broad chest.

So, here is the problem. With all his time being spent on hunting and fishing and enjoying nature, Esau spent little time sharpening his people skills. Chatting with friends about nothing special, dropping by a friend's house to discuss what had been going on that week, and really even talking at all seemed a little frivolous to Esau.

He appears to have lived for the moment and the satisfaction of his primary needs. There doesn't seem to have been much else in his life. How do I know this? Listen to this part of the story:

Esau was a twin. His brother Jacob is described by contrasting the two men. While Esau spent his time outdoors hunting, Jacob spent his time with his family, especially his mother. When Esau was hunting for the animal of the season, Jacob was discussing life and how to live it better. One day when Esau returned home following a day in the wild, he smelled something really good that his brother Jacob was cooking. When Esau asked for some, Jacob said he would give Esau some, but for a price. It would cost him his birthright.

A birthright was the means of passing all of the family inheritance down to the eldest son. They did not do wills at this time in history nor did they equally divide up things among all the children. Everything went to the oldest son. Everyone else, whether it was one sibling or 15, got nothing. According to birth order, Esau was the one to inherit everything. Even though the two brothers were twins, Esau came out first. (Ask any set of twins today who is the oldest, and they will still both know...to the minute!!)

Well, back to the story. Esau, realizing that a birthright wouldn't feed him right then, gave it up to Jacob. Esau traded his entire inheritance for a bowl of stew! Yep, Esau lived for the moment. He made decisions based on his basic needs and not the big picture. Now, before you go out and really think that Esau is an idiot....

Have you ever cheated in the moment, not thinking about the consequences later?

Have you ever given in to a temptation or a lustful situation, not taking into account the possible effects of your one moment of passion?

We may not be too much unlike Esau after all!

Viewed in this light, we can see why God was so displeased when Esau was careless and flippant about his inheritance. We can also see why it was such a big deal for Esau to think of himself as being above the needs of maintaining the family inheritance established by God. No one, however capable or "tough" is self-sufficient and above the need for meaningful relationships—either with other people or with God.

But let me finish the story for you...

Jacob was quite the manipulator (a story for another day) and toward the end of his father's life, he pulled one more trick. He and his mother Rebekah tricked Isaac into blessing the wrong son! Now, back in those days, the father's blessing was both spiritual and physical. The father of each family had one family blessing to pass on and once that blessing was given, there was nothing else to give. We know this because, after a very complicated trick, Isaac blessed Jacob thinking he was Esau. Once Esau came in to be blessed and Isaac realized that he had already given his blessing to the wrong son, he said that he had no more blessing to give Esau.

Now, although parents nowadays don't have some kind of miraculous giving of a blessing, think about these things:

Were you the favorite child who got all of one parent's attention? Did you ever feel like you got completely left out and overlooked?

Were you the child of a blended family who never felt like you fit in the new family? Did you truly feel like a step-child and carry that pain with you into adult life?

Having favorites and manipulating others for affection carry serious repercussions. Even in our story, the two brothers stayed separated for twenty years before making peace with each other. Ever have that feeling?

No one of us is tough enough to live alone. None of us wants to be overlooked and left out. Tricking others for affection or love doesn't usually end up well! Work on your people skills. Evaluate your relationships. Learn to say I love you and I need you. That takes a true man!

Challenge:

This week, spend time evaluating your relationships and look for ways to express your love and need for your family. Focus on learning to be more caring, gentle and patient in your relationships...

Discussion Questions:

1. Which brother in the story do you most resemble? Why?

2. In what ways has your search to be a "man's man" hurt your relationships
    a. With your wife
    b. With your children
    c. With your guy friends
    d. With church members?

3. Spend some time discussing in your group how your ideas of masculinity have changed over time. (Note to the young men here- Listen carefully to older men in the group who have grown children and now grandchildren and how this has effected them in their view of being a "man's man.") Can you still be masculine and be more caring? More gentle with others? More patient?

Onan
Pleasure without Responsibility
Genesis 38: 8-10

8 Then Judah said to Er's brother Onan, "Go and marry Tamar, as our law requires of the brother of a man who has died. You must produce an heir for your brother."

9 But Onan was not willing to have a child who would not be his own heir. So whenever he had intercourse with his brother's wife, he spilled the semen on the ground. This prevented her from having a child who would belong to his brother. 10 But the LORD considered it evil for Onan to deny a child to his dead brother. So the LORD took Onan's life, too.

This Old Testament story is a little strange for our time and culture, but let me explain the reasoning behind it...and I think you will get the point.

God's laws were put in place so that no one was ever excluded from His care and protection. That is, unless someone blatantly chooses to live in sin instead of doing what God says. An example of this care is found in the law regarding the protection of women in the Old Testament. At first read, the law regarding heirs seems to be a law about property being handed down from father to offspring. However, the law provided for the care of women in particular. If there were no offspring (sons) linked to property, there would be no one to take care of women left behind.

Such is the case here. Judah, one of Jacob's twelve sons, had sons named Er, Onan, and Shelah. Er married Tamar, but because he was wicked, the Lord took his life. According to the law at that time, Onan was supposed to marry Tamar, and their first son would be Er's heir. That would ensure the property stayed with Tamar and her son. That son would then take care of his mother in her old age. This process would prevent what always happened to women who did not have someone to care for them—they become either destitute beggars or prostitutes.

Onan refused to comply with this law of God's.

Now, in our day, it would be more than strange taking a brother's wife like this...not to mention bigomy! But think back to the times and get the point here. Read on in the section of scripture. Onan took all the pleasures of having Tamar as his wife. He just wouldn't give her a son to be his father's heir, going out of his way not to impregnate her.

He chose to take the sexual pleasures without assuming the consequences and/or responsibilities. So God took Onan's life as well.

There are several things in this story that displeased God. I'm not sure which one may have made God more angry:

There's the refusal to do what the law said to do.
There's the total disregard of taking care of a woman.
There's the seeking of sexual pleasure without any regard
   for the accompanying responsibility.
And, quite frankly, there just the unwillingness to help a
   brother out.

I'm reminded of the parable in the New Testament in Luke 10: 30-37 about the Good Samaritan.

30 Jesus replied with a story: "A Jewish man was traveling on a trip from Jerusalem to Jericho, and he was attacked by bandits. They stripped him of his clothes, beat him up, and left him half dead beside the road.

31 "By chance a priest came along. But when he saw the man lying there, he crossed to the other side of the road and passed him by. 32 A Temple assistant[b] walked over and looked at him lying there, but he also passed by on the other side.

33 "Then a despised Samaritan came along, and when he saw the man, he felt compassion for him. 34 Going over to him, the Samaritan soothed his wounds with olive oil and wine and bandaged them. Then he put the man on his own donkey and took him to an inn, where he took care of him. 35 The next day he handed the innkeeper two silver coins,[c] telling him, 'Take care of this man. If his bill runs higher than this, I'll pay you the next time I'm here.'

36 "Now which of these three would you say was a neighbor to the man who was attacked by bandits?" Jesus asked.

37 The man replied, "The one who showed him mercy." Then Jesus said, "Yes, now go and do the same."

In this story, two somewhat religious men pass up helping a man in obvious need by thinking that whatever they had previously planned was more important than a "brother in need." The story's hero is a half-breed loser of society, who not only assumes responsibility for the injured man, but also goes the second mile- taking him to be cared for and paying for the expenses, no questions asked. This story is told to a group of really important religious dudes who had asked the question, "Who is my neighbor?" Well, Jesus answers them with a challenge to see all those in need around them as neighbors. This whole thing started when those same religious guys had tried to trick Jesus by asking him what the most important law was. You see they kept the law, at least their version of it, and seemed to be willing to be put to the test. Jesus tells them that the law is really just summed up in two major requests of God:

1. Love God with all your heart and
2. Love your neighbor as yourself.

So here we have Jesus' cliff notes of the entire Bible. The problem with fulfilling it is that we sometimes have to do things we don't want to do. And sometimes we have to do it with people we don't want to do it with.

We circle back around to Onan. He wasn't willing to do what God wanted him to do and he wasn't willing to do it with someone he didn't want to do it with. So he died.

Are you dying spiritually for the same reasons?

Challenge:
This week, focus on the women in your life. How can you be more respectful of them?

Discussion Questions:

1. Why do you think Onan might not have wanted to help his brother out? Is it possible that this was an issue with his brother or is it always an issue with God?

2. What were you taught about women growing up? In what ways have you had to learn how to better respect and treat women? Give examples.

3. Name one area of your life in which you struggle with doing what God really wants you to do. Share it with the group.

4. As men we all struggle with some form of sexual temptation. Whether it is lust, an affair, inappropriate talking, or just getting too close to another female other than our wife, we all struggle. Discuss as much of this as you are comfortable with the men in your group. You do not have to confess sins here if you do not feel comfortable doing so. Share the area of temptation that is most prevalent in your life.

Joseph
God Leads my Life
Genesis 45: 1-8

Joseph could stand it no longer. There were many people in the room, and he said to his attendants, "Out, all of you!" So he was alone with his brothers when he told them who he was. 2 Then he broke down and wept. He wept so loudly the Egyptians could hear him, and word of it quickly carried to Pharaoh's palace.

3 "I am Joseph!" he said to his brothers. "Is my father still alive?" But his brothers were speechless! They were stunned to realize that Joseph was standing there in front of them. 4 "Please, come closer," he said to them. So they came closer. And he said again, "I am Joseph, your brother, whom you sold into slavery in Egypt. 5 But don't be upset, and don't be angry with yourselves for selling me to this place. It was God who sent me here ahead of you to preserve your lives. 6 This famine that has ravaged the land for two years will last five more years, and there will be neither plowing nor harvesting. 7 God has sent me ahead of you to keep you and your families alive and to preserve many survivors 8 So it was God who sent me here, not you! And he is the one who made me an adviser to Pharaoh—the manager of his entire palace and the governor of all Egypt.

We first meet Joseph and his brothers in Genesis 37. They are all sons of the same father, Jacob, but all have different mothers. Because of the favoritism shown by Jacob to his one wife, Rachel, Joseph and Benjamin become the favored children as these are the only two sons she had. Long before Benjamin comes on the scene, Jacob blatantly favors Joseph. Being very unwise in favoring one son over another one, Jacob fosters jealousy and strife between the other sons.

If you ever went to Bible classes growing up as a child (or saw the play Joseph and the Amazing Technicolor Dream Coat) you know that dad gives Joseph a special gift. Interpreting the Old Testament in this story may indeed be correct to make this a coat of many colors. It might also be accurate to suggest that the coat was indeed long sleeved. What difference would that make? Men generally wore sleeveless tunics (much like our muscle shirts of today) in order to be able to work without being hindered. Nothing is worse than getting a sleeve caught in the ax while you are chopping wood! Men, or boys, who were wealthy, or spoiled, did not have to worry about that. They could wear long sleeved coats, as it is difficult to get a sleeve caught up in pointing to others about what you want them to do for you. Whether it is a long sleeve coat or a coat of many colors, the same principle applies. Only wealthy people could afford colored materials and especially as a young child.

Well, you get the picture. One spoiled brother and all the other poor slob sons doing all the work. You can imagine how they felt about him. Angry is not strong enough. As we enter the story here, blind jealousy and rage are present. Let's continue...

One day as Joseph carried lunch to his brothers while they tended the flocks, the brothers decided to kill him. As they were plotting this, maybe struggling with just a twinge of guilt, they noticed a caravan of travelers going to Egypt. What a stroke of luck!! They decided to sell Joseph for 20 pieces of silver-getting rid of a spoiled brother and pocketing a little cash at the same time. Having finished this business deal, they took Joseph's special coat, dipped it in goat's blood and took it to their father, telling him that Joseph had been killed by a wild animal. If you have ever seen a man wild with jealousy act like an animal....well, at least part of the story was partly true.

Jacob was heart broken, devastated, literally at a loss to know what to do.

Well, time goes on as it usually does after tragic things. Joseph is being blessed by God with special gifts and friends in high places. It isn't long before Joseph is in charge of the greatest food market in the world. Egypt has the only food and they have stored enough for themselves and enough left over to sell to other countries during 7 years of famine! Either there is a string of completely coincidental occasions that work together so perfectly for this story.....or wait-maybe God has orchestrated the whole thing!

Meanwhile back at the ranch, Jacob and his family are experiencing the famine. Caravan traffic has brought news that Egypt has all the food anyone could want! Jacob sends his sons to Egypt with money and instructions to buy enough food to keep his family alive. The same brothers who had sold Joseph into slavery now end up face to face with him buying grain.

Joseph of course recognizes his brothers immediately. They have no clue who he is. How would they? In their wildest dreams, they would not have imagined ever seeing their brother overseeing the biggest Egyptian market in history. They would not have recognized him with the Egyptian eye makeup either that royalty wore back then!! Anyway, after a series of "toying" with them, making them come back and forth, he orders his attendants to leave him and his brothers alone. He begins to weep so loudly that his cries and sobs are heard throughout the palace, carrying news to the Pharoah.

Joseph at this point reveals his identity to his brothers and inquires of the health of his father. The brothers are shocked and frightened. I mean, wouldn't you be? Not only for seeing your brother in Egyptian royal robes, but also having the power to put you to death on the spot?

Here's what the brothers have missed, and this is the entire point of the story. God has worked in Joseph's life through all these years, through all kinds of strange and sometimes uncomfortable situations and through the sculpting of a heart. God had been active in the life of Joseph. He had not been as active in the lives of the other brothers.

You see, it's difficult for God to be working in the life of a person who has so much hatred, jealousy, guilt and pain as the other brothers had.

And here is Joseph's response to them as they stutter and shift from one foot to the other, wanting to run away, but too afraid to move. He tells them to not be angry with themselves! Not only is HE not angry with them, he assures them that they should not be angry with themselves! How could Joseph ever have gotten to a place of peace and forgiveness?

He had seen the handiwork of God. He trusted that God had a plan. It was God's plan from the beginning to work this out. Wouldn't we all be happier, more peaceful and less resentful if we trusted that God is in charge of our lives too? The very things we have gone through may have been there for something we will not see or understand until another day.

To end the story, Joseph brings all his family to Egypt to live throughout the famine. In fact, they reside there for about 400 years until Charlton Heston, (that's Moses) leads them to the land of Canaan.

Just consider…what might God be preparing you for in the near future if you will just let Him take control of you?

Challenge:
This week, focus on trying to see ways in which God is leading you in your life—-and to what purpose. You might be surprised.

Discussion Questions

1. Have you ever thought that God might be preparing you for something?

2. Think of a time or event that you did not understand while you were going through it, that when you looked back on it, you are sure God had a hand in. Share this with others in the group.

3. Why do you struggle with letting God be in control of your life? In fact, isn't it against a man's "nature" to give up control to others to "fix things?"

4. What estrangements (separations from other people) have you dealt with in your life? How did you grieve over them? How did you handle the anger/rage? The forgiveness? The reconciliation?

5. In what ways have you decided to follow God's lead instead of your own? In what specific areas of your life? Which ones are easier for you to let go of?

Moses
But I can't do that!
Exodus 3:11- 4:13

11 But Moses protested to God, "Who am I to appear before Pharaoh? Who am I to lead the people of Israel out of Egypt?"

12 God answered, "I will be with you. And this is your sign that I am the one who has sent you: When you have brought the people out of Egypt, you will worship God at this very mountain."

13 But Moses protested, "If I go to the people of Israel and tell them, 'The God of your ancestors has sent me to you,' they will ask me, 'What is his name?' Then what should I tell them?"

14 God replied to Moses, "I AM WHO I AM[J] *Say this to the people of Israel: I AM has sent me to you." 15 God also said to Moses, "Say this to the people of Israel: Yahweh*[J] *the God of your ancestors—the God of Abraham, the God of Isaac, and the God of Jacob—has sent me to you. This is my eternal name, my name to remember for all generations.*

16 "Now go and call together all the elders of Israel. Tell them, 'The LORD, the God of your ancestors—the God of Abraham, Isaac, and Jacob—has appeared to me. He told me, "I have been watching closely, and I see how the Egyptians are treating you. 17 I have promised to rescue you from your oppression in Egypt. I will lead you to a land flowing with milk and honey—the land where the Canaanites, Hittites, Amorites, Perizzites, Hivites, and Jebusites now live."'

18 "The elders of Israel will accept your message. Then you and the elders must go to the king of Egypt and tell him, 'The Lord, the God of the Hebrews, has met with us. So please let us take a three-day journey into the wilderness to offer sacrifices to the Lord, our God.'

19 "But I know that the king of Egypt will not let you go unless a mighty hand forces him 20 So I will raise my hand and strike the Egyptians, performing all kinds of miracles among them. Then at last he will let you go. 21 And I will cause the Egyptians to look favorably on you. They will give you gifts when you go so you will not leave empty-handed. 22 Every Israelite woman will ask for articles of silver and gold and fine clothing from her Egyptian neighbors and from the foreign women in their houses. You will dress your sons and daughters with these, stripping the Egyptians of their wealth."

Exodus 4
1 But Moses protested again, "What if they won't believe me or listen to me? What if they say, 'The Lord never appeared to you'?"
2 Then the Lord asked him, "What is that in your hand?"
"A shepherd's staff," Moses replied.
3 "Throw it down on the ground," the Lord told him. So Moses threw down the staff, and it turned into a snake! Moses jumped back.

4 Then the LORD told him, "Reach out and grab its tail." So Moses reached out and grabbed it, and it turned back into a shepherd's staff in his hand.

5 "Perform this sign," the LORD told him. "Then they will believe that the LORD, the God of their ancestors — the God of Abraham, the God of Isaac, and the God of Jacob — really has appeared to you."

6 Then the LORD said to Moses, "Now put your hand inside your cloak." So Moses put his hand inside his cloak, and when he took it out again, his hand was white as snow with a severe skin disease. 7 "Now put your hand back into your cloak," the LORD said. So Moses put his hand back in, and when he took it out again, it was as healthy as the rest of his body.

8 The LORD said to Moses, "If they do not believe you and are not convinced by the first miraculous sign, they will be convinced by the second sign. 9 And if they don't believe you or listen to you even after these two signs, then take some water from the Nile River and pour it out on the dry ground. When you do, the water from the Nile will turn to blood on the ground."

10 But Moses pleaded with the LORD, "O Lord, I'm not very good with words. I never have been, and I'm not now, even though you have spoken to me. I get tongue-tied, and my words get tangled."

11 Then the LORD asked Moses, "Who makes a person's mouth? Who decides whether people speak or do not speak, hear or do not hear, see or do not see? Is it not I, the LORD? 12 Now go! I will be with you as you speak, and I will instruct you in what to say."

13 But Moses again pleaded, "Lord, please! Send anyone else."

Moses, after being set afloat on the Nile River in a basket, was rescued by Pharoah's daughter and raised in Pharoah's palace. In fact, he was raised with all the privileges and power of a child of Pharoah. After growing to manhood in Egypt, Moses learned his true identity as an Israelite, killed an Egyptian for hurting an Israelite, and was banished to the wilderness. While crossing the wilderness, he arrived at the well of Jethro of Midian where he eventually married, had sons and lived for the next 40 years.

One day while tending the flocks at the foot of Mt. Sinai, he sees a really weird thing. There is this bush that is on fire, but it is not being burned up. When he investigates further, God speaks to him from the burning bush! Now this bush is REALLY becoming weird! God tells him from the bush Who He is and that Moses should remove his sandals from his feet because he is standing on holy ground. This is the beginning of a conversation between God and Moses in which God tells Moses He has heard the cries of his slave people in Egypt. They had been there in the Land of Goshen since the time of Joseph. Remember that story previously? Anyway, now they have outgrown their welcome because God has blessed them with numbers and strength. Pharoahs don't usually like for other nations to be stronger than themselves...especially in their own land. So he had made them slaves. The point today? God told Moses He had chosen him to lead his people out of the land of Egypt.

As you can imagine, Moses would have NO desire to return to the land of Egypt. He lived a life that wasn't his to live and took a life that wasn't his to take. Yes, let's go right back into that! Anyway, as you can imagine, Moses started making excuses. They are pretty flimsy ones too if you reread the text above.

Moses begins to rattle off his excuses to God. God gives a declaration of Who He is and promises to watch over Moses and the children of Israel. In fact, God promises that He will cause the Egyptians to treat the Israelites well and load them up with wealth and provisions. Not to be distracted from his excuse-giving, Moses continues.

Excuse after excuse Moses states. Excuse after excuse, God gives His response. In fact, God gives Moses miraculous signs to help convince the Egyptians that He means what He says. Or were they for Moses to realize that? Either way, he is armed with some pretty stout miracles.

By the end of the conversation, Moses is scraping the bottom of the excuse barrel. He tells God that he is not a good speaker.

Now we know that Moses was trained in the house of Pharoah and educated in the highest of arts and knowledge. It is highly unlikely that Moses had a speech problem....maybe cold feet, but not an inability to speak well.

The final statement on Moses' part is the real issue. He pleads with God to just send someone else. Bottom line: we don't always want to do what God is calling us to do. Making excuses may get us out of doing things around the house, or around the church or even with some of our closest friends....but with God?? Let's finish the story.

It is important to realize here that God does not let Moses off the hook. He does not let Moses reject His call. Yes, God gets angry here and would have been justified in pulling Moses into the burning bush. Instead, He gives him the help he needs, to do what God is calling him to do. In this case, God sends Aaron. Note for those of you who have heard this entire story before. Aaron plays a small part in what God has called Moses to do. To Moses' credit, he steps up and really does fulfill God's desire.

For us, it might be important to realize that God calls us to do things- specific things with and through our lives. Refusing is an option, but not for God. Take the promise of God seriously from this story. "I will be with you."

Think about it. How many excuses have you given to Him? How many times has He had to listen to your weak and pitiful excuses for not doing what He wants you to do?

Challenge:
Spend sometime this week challenging yourself to work harder at the "doing" and less at the "avoiding."

Discussion Questions

1. Make a list of 5 excuses you have made to God below. These can focus on any area of your life, including, but not limited to:

    Your involvement in church

    Your being a better husband or father

    Increasing your prayer life, your commitment to God and your acts of service to others

    Turning up your spiritual enthusiasm

2. With each of the 5 excuses, write a commitment to begin fulfilling what you really think God has called you to do.

    -
    -
    -
    -
    -

3. Discuss with your group how you intend to accomplish these commitments this time. Ask if someone in the group, or the group itself, would act as accountability partners for you in your goals.

Pharaoh
Choosing to Have a Hard Heart
Exodus 7-9

3 But I will make Pharaoh's heart stubborn so I can multiply my miraculous signs and wonders in the land of Egypt. 4 Even then Pharaoh will refuse to listen to you. So I will bring down my fist on Egypt. Then I will rescue my forces—my people, the Israelites—from the land of Egypt with great acts of judgment. 5 When I raise my powerful hand and bring out the Israelites, the Egyptians will know that I am the LORD."

In the last verse above, we see that the Lord hardened Pharaoh's heart. That ultimately leads to the destruction of not only Pharaoh himself, but also most of his army. For those of us who believe that God is loving, merciful and not willing that any should perish, we are left with a quandary that is not easily answered. How can God deliberately turn someone's heart to stone and cause that person to make choices that ultimately lead to his destruction? At first, this seems totally contradictory to everything we know about God and His divine will. Is God really being harsh here or is there another explanation that we may have over-looked?

Between the chapters of Exodus 7 and 9, we are told that Pharaoh hardened his OWN heart at least 6 times when dealing with the Israelites! Six times as Moses and Aaron asked to let the Israelites go from the land of Egypt, Pharaoh hardened his heart. Time after time,

Pharaoh has dealt with the plagues sent by God. As God attempts to REVEAL His awesome power, He really tries to communicate that He means what He says.

Pharaoh must begin to think that either he can outlast God or that God's power has its limitations. You ever been there?

Pharaoh must have begun to think of himself as all-powerful, almost god-like, and above any plague God could send. But we know that at judgment day, "every knee will bow and every tongue confess that Jesus is Lord." Romans 14:11 Pharaoh had to come to the realization that God is God alone, and that he—Pharaoh—is NOT! It is important that we are very clear here. God did not begin to harden Pharaoh's heart until after Pharaoh had made the choice himself to have a rock-hard heart.

Sometimes God uses situations surrounding the choices we have made to display His own glory. A case in point is the story of Jesus' best friend Lazarus in John 11. When Jesus heard that Lazarus was sick, he waited four days before beginning the journey to his friend's side. When he got there, he was told by his two sisters that it was too late. Their brother was dead and buried. Jesus had disappointed them. Jesus, however, explained to them that this had happened just to be a display of God's power. In fact, showing the glory in this way could not possibly be misinterpreted as anything but God's complete and indisputable power...not coincidence, not happenstance, unlike anything anyone had ever seen. Not only was Lazarus dead, but he had been dead for four days. Well, the end of the story was that Jesus called Lazarus out of the grave....and he came! The point of the story was that some things are done so that God's glory can be shown to others. There should be no doubt that God is the worker of these great events and that He is the One who deserves all the glory and praise.

Now back to our first story. This is the case with Pharaoh. It was only after Pharaoh's idolatrous, pagan heart was hardened significantly by his own choices that God began to harden it even more. Each time his heart was hardened, a new plague was unleashed. God's miraculous glory was unfolding and being shown to be greater than anything Pharaoh's magicians could do...and more than any Egyptian could have imagined possible!

In addition, God was using this time and set of events to fulfill prophesies and promises given to Abraham centuries before. In Genesis 15:13-15, God tells Abraham that the descendents would be freed after being enslaved for 400 years AND that they would come out of slavery with great wealth. By God completing the process, and by hardening Pharaoh's heart also, the Egyptians were so sick of the Israelites and the plagues, they were willing to give up nearly everything just to have them gone! Also in the same passage, God told Abraham that He would punish the enslavers. So the plagues and subsequent chariot race into the Red Sea were a fulfillment of that promise. Had the process not been completed to God's needed result, there would have been no frantic pursuit and no Israelites with their backs to the sea. We would have missed seeing the wonderful evidence of God's glory, power and deliverance. Wow! Just imagine what we would have missed!

So we learn from this:

God allows us to choose whether we will be hard-hearted or not.
He will not override our choice, but He may very well use our bad ones for His own purposes.
We must suffer the consequences of our choices.

Think about this. Pharaoh's hard-hearted choices led to his destruction and the destruction of many of his people. Your choices don't have to be that way. Choose to glorify God with your choices.

Challenge:
This week, give some thought to the status of your heart condition as you make your choices. Are they glorifying to you or to God?

Discussion Questions:

1. What kind of heart do you think you have before God?

2. Have you made hard-hearted choices? How have these choices led you down the wrong path? With what results? Were relationships destroyed in the process?

3. How have these choices affected your family and your ability to be the head of the household?

4. Can you think of ways in which God has been glorified by your good choices?

Gideon
God's Waiting on You
Judges 6:11-40

11 Then the angel of the Lord came and sat beneath the great tree at Ophrah, which belonged to Joash of the clan of Abiezer. Gideon son of Joash was threshing wheat at the bottom of a winepress to hide the grain from the Midianites. 12 The angel of the Lord appeared to him and said, "Mighty hero, the Lord is with you!"

13 "Sir," Gideon replied, "if the Lord is with us, why has all this happened to us? And where are all the miracles our ancestors told us about? Didn't they say, 'The Lord brought us up out of Egypt'? But now the Lord has abandoned us and handed us over to the Midianites."

14 Then the Lord turned to him and said, "Go with the strength you have, and rescue Israel from the Midianites. I am sending you!"

15 "But Lord," Gideon replied, "how can I rescue Israel? My clan is the weakest in the whole tribe of Manasseh, and I am the least in my entire family!"

16 The LORD said to him, "I will be with you. And you will destroy the Midianites as if you were fighting against one man."

17 Gideon replied, "If you are truly going to help me, show me a sign to prove that it is really the LORD speaking to me. 18 Don't go away until I come back and bring my offering to you." He answered, "I will stay here until you return."

19 Gideon hurried home. He cooked a young goat, and with a basket of flour he baked some bread without yeast. Then, carrying the meat in a basket and the broth in a pot, he brought them out and presented them to the angel, who was under the great tree.

20 The angel of God said to him, "Place the meat and the unleavened bread on this rock, and pour the broth over it." And Gideon did as he was told. 21 Then the angel of the LORD touched the meat and bread with the tip of the staff in his hand, and fire flamed up from the rock and consumed all he had brought. And the angel of the LORD disappeared.

22 When Gideon realized that it was the angel of the LORD, he cried out, "Oh, Sovereign LORD, I'm doomed! I have seen the angel of the LORD face to face!"

23 "It is all right," the LORD replied. "Do not be afraid. You will not die." 24 And Gideon built an altar to the LORD there and named it Yahweh-Shalom (which means "the LORD is peace"). The altar remains in Ophrah in the land of the clan of Abiezer to this day.

25 That night the LORD said to Gideon, "Take the second bull from your father's herd, the one that is seven years old. Pull down your father's altar to Baal, and cut down the Asherah pole standing beside it. 26 Then build an altar to the LORD your God here on this hilltop sanctuary, laying the stones carefully. Sacrifice the bull as a burnt offering on the altar, using as fuel the wood of the Asherah pole you cut down."

27 So Gideon took ten of his servants and did as the LORD had commanded. But he did it at night because he was afraid of the other members of his father's household and the people of the town.

36 Then Gideon said to God, "If you are truly going to use me to rescue Israel as you promised, 37 prove it to me in this way. I will put a wool fleece on the threshing floor tonight. If the fleece is wet with dew in the morning but the ground is dry, then I will know that you are going to help me rescue Israel as you promised." 38 And that is just what happened. When Gideon got up early the next morning, he squeezed the fleece and wrung out a whole bowlful of water.

39 Then Gideon said to God, "Please don't be angry with me, but let me make one more request. Let me use the fleece for one more test. This time let the fleece remain dry while the ground around it is wet with dew." 40 So that night God did as Gideon asked. The fleece was dry in the morning, but the ground was covered with dew.

It seems like that every time you turn around, the people of the Old Testament are crying out to God for something. Faced with hunger in the land of Midian, they cry out to God in our story today. God answers their cries by sending an angel with a message to Gideon, calling him to be a hero.

God gives the message to Gideon that he is the one God has chosen to rescue the people in this situation. When Gideon inquires as to how God intends to do this, God assures him that He will strengthen Gideon so much that the battle will be as easy as if Gideon were only fighting one man. This sounds really good to Gideon, but he wants a little more. He asks this miraculous Being to prove His identity by staying in place—-sitting under a tree—- while Gideon goes to get an offering. And the Lord agrees! Imagine that—God waited on Gideon, sitting around like He had nothing else better to do but to hang out and wait for someone to believe in Him! I wonder if God does that kind of thing for us today?

Gideon hurries home and prepares a meal for the Lord and carries it back to the tree where the angel of God is waiting. When he arrives, the angel of the Lord tells Gideon to put the food he has brought on the rock and pour broth over it. Of course, now that it's all wet, the offering should not burn up, but when the angel touches the food with his staff, it bursts into flames and is consumed. Then the angel disappears.

At this, Gideon realizes that the angel of the Lord is truly an angel of the Lord, and he becomes frightened. I mean, you don't ask God or His angel to stick around while you make up your mind if you believe in Him, right? Well, God tells Gideon not to be afraid because fortunately God's patience with us is always better then our patience with Him!

Gideon is on fire for God (no pun intended) and is willing to do what God tells him to do. His first chore is to knock down the altar the people had built to Baal, a false god, and the Asherah poles used in false worship. Gideon did it and built an altar to God in that same place, using the Asherah pole as wood for his sacrifice to God! Note here that once Gideon got the message from God, he was willing to do it.

One day, the spirit of God overtook Gideon and he blew a horn that was a call to arms for all the tribes of Israel. As the armies began to gather, Gideon asked God to verify His call and His promise. Now pause for just a moment. Hadn't God already proven Himself to Gideon? Why did Gideon need additional proof? Is this a lack of faith or a sign for himself AND others that God was in charge? We are not sure from the story.

Gideon asked God to cause dew to fall on the fleece lying on the ground, but for the ground to be dry. The next morning, it had happened! Gideon was happy that this had happened, but probably started questioning the circumstances. Was it a coincidence? Is it possible that this hadn't happened from God? What if he was reading too much into this whole sign thing? You ever been there? Have you ever asked God for something and when it happened, second guessed yourself? It's not as if you aren't willing to do what God wants you to do, but you just want to be sure!

Well, that's where Gideon found himself. So, he asked God not to be angry at him if he asked for one more sign. Pause here for a moment in the story to note Gideon's attitude. It was one of humility and openness, not demanding and doubting. When we ask God to lead us and need a little more assurance, we have story after story in the Bible of God being willing to do that for us. When we ask as if we deserve it or really don't want to do it anyway, God may not have the patience we want Him to have!

Gideon asks God to have the fleece be dry and the ground wet the next morning, and it happened. You might not be a person who believes in "signs" from God, in the sense that you can ask for God to do a little magic in front of your eyes to communicate something to you. I would say to you that God has no desire to be a little magician, but He does have a desire to get your attention and to lead you. You might look in any of the following ways to see how God might be sending you a message sign:

1. A sense of complete calm and peace about a decision you are wrestling with.
2. Someone out of the blue saying something to you confirming a choice you need to make.
3. A specific request being granted that could be "coincidence" but you asked for it to happen.
4. An open door that you walk through, leading you to another opportunity and another and another until you see the end result.
5. A Biblical example of a story or principle that applies directly to your situation.

Regardless of how you feel about miraculous signs, God does want to be in charge of your everyday life. Gideon showed us, that with a proper attitude, God is willing to do what we ask....when we are willing to do what He asks from us!

Challenge:
This week experiment with praying more to God in asking for His leading your life. Don't let a decision be made that is not bathed in prayer with Him.

Discussion Questions:

1. How do you think God speaks to you? Discuss and explore the options:
   a. Through His Word
   b. Through other people
   c. Through special circumstances or blessings
   d. In attention-getting circumstances or conditions
   e. With signs properly asked for and interpreted
   f. Others

2. Once you have explored the above options, discuss in your group how you may have had an answer to a request from God with the other men in your group.

3. How much reliance on God's leading of your life do you have?

4. Were you taught to pray for God to show you what He wanted you to do in your day-to-day life? How do you feel about that?

5. Some people believe that God sends His angels to us today to protect us, guide us, challenge us and to encourage us. Have you ever had a situation happen in your life that may have included a special, unexplainable person in it? Share it with others in your group.

Jephthah
Be Careful Making Promises You Can't Keep
Judges 11:29-40

*29 At that time the Spirit of the L*ORD *came upon Jephthah, and he went throughout the land of Gilead and Manasseh, including Mizpah in Gilead, and from there he led an army against the Ammonites. 30 And Jephthah made a vow to the L*ORD*. He said, "If you give me victory over the Ammonites, 31 I will give to the L*ORD *whatever comes out of my house to meet me when I return in triumph. I will sacrifice it as a burnt offering."*

*32 So Jephthah led his army against the Ammonites, and the L*ORD *gave him victory. 33 He crushed the Ammonites, devastating about twenty towns from Aroer to an area near Minnith and as far away as Abel-keramim. In this way Israel defeated the Ammonites.*

34 When Jephthah returned home to Mizpah, his daughter came out to meet him, playing on a tambourine and dancing for joy. She was his one and only child; he had no other sons or daughters. 35 When he saw her, he tore his clothes in anguish. "Oh, my daughter!" he cried out. "You have completely destroyed me! You've brought disaster on *me! For I have made a vow to the L*ORD*, and I cannot take it back."*

*36 And she said, "Father, if you have made a vow to the L*ORD*, you must do to me what you have vowed, for the L*ORD *has given you a great victory over your enemies, the Ammonites. 37 But first let me do this one thing: Let me go up and roam in the hills and weep with my friends for two months, because I will die a virgin."*

38 "You may go," Jephthah said. And he sent her away for two months. She and her friends went into the hills and wept because she would never have children. 39 When she returned home, her father kept the vow he had made, and she died a virgin.
So it has become a custom in Israel 40 for young Israelite women to go away for four days each year to lament the fate of Jephthah's daughter.

In a way, it's one of the oddest stories in the Old Testament. Understanding it may take some work on our part, but let's do it!

Many times in the Old Testament, it is said that the "spirit of the Lord" comes upon a man. Although it is never really explained what that means, in nearly every case in which this happens, whoever receives the Spirit of God does some great and heroic thing. It appears that God wanted desperately to help mankind out- to the point of living inside of him in order for him to experience the power of God. In the New Testament, we also have the Spirit of God living inside of us, but it is not something that comes upon someone just prior to performing a specific act of courage or heroism. Instead, according to *Acts 2:38-39:*

Peter replied, "Repent and be baptized every one of you in the name of Jesus Christ for the forgiveness of your sins. And you will receive the gift of the Holy Spirit. The promise is for you and your children and for all who are far off—for all whom the Lord our God will call."

And again in ***Galatians 4:6***, Paul refers to something we have received from God.

Because you are sons, God sent the Spirit of his Son into our hearts, the Spirit who calls out, "Abba, Father."

We seem to have the ability to "house" God within our own bodies, generally referred to in religious studies as the "indwelling of the Spirit. Well, I suppose the way it was done in the Old Testament was sometimes more exciting, but the promise of how it is done in the New Testament is certainly more reassuring. Having the Spirit of God living within us is a seal or covenant between God and man that God has saved him. THAT is a pretty good thing!

Anyway, back to our story.

Jephthah was a man of God who had a pretty good reputation for doing what was right in the sight of God. One day, the Spirit of God came upon him and he was empowered to lead the army of Israel against the Ammonites. Before defeating the Ammonites, he made a vow to God. Now this is where he both showed his faith and started to get himself into trouble. Let me explain…

God had not asked for a commitment or a "deal" from Jepthah. Jepthah was apparently not asking for a sign as in the case of a previous lesson we have studied together. God values commitments from people. Perhaps that is because God always keeps His promises to us! As soon as Jepthah made this vow, God intended for him to keep it. Hence, the rest of his story…

Jepthah made a vow to God that if God would give him this victory, he would offer the first thing coming out of his house on his return home as a burnt offering sacrifice to the Lord. Well, God gave him his victory. In fact, Jepthah led the Israelites through twenty towns and defeated the Ammonites in all of them. Jepthah was a happy man as he traveled home in victory.

When he returned home, his joy quickly turned to anguish as the first thing to come out of his house and meet him was his beloved daughter, his only child. Now, quick note here: animals lived in the house, on the bottom floor of most homes during Bible days.

Offering the first thing most likely referred to any animal that ran out of the house, even the most favorite animal or house "pet." Who would have ever thought that the first thing out would be a human being? And his only daughter??

In his grief, he explained to his daughter that he had made a vow to God and couldn't take it back. Watch the response here... She agreed that he should keep his vow to God! What kind of faith existed in this household? Can you even imagine someone sacrificing an only child because of a promise made? (Oh, yea, maybe God sacrificing Jesus because of the promise He made to save the world!)

The daughter did ask for two months to go to the hills and weep with her friends because she was to die a virgin. Jepthah agreed and most likely spent the same number of days weeping himself. BUT, when she returned, he sacrificed her to God.

It's a hard story, but in many ways models the story of what God did for us through Jesus. I am glad that God did not go back on His promise, aren't you?

God expects the same from you today.

Challenge:
This week consider how committed we are with our promises.
Begin following through no matter how hard it is!

Discussion Questions

1. Evaluate the commitment level of your home right now. Does your household model the spiritual level of Jepthah's? What are things Jepthah must have done in order to raise a faithful daughter like his?

2. Make a list of the commitments you hold to others below, being as specific as you want to be.
   a. To your wife

   b. To your children

   c. To your job

   d. To your friends

   e. To your church family

   f. To yourself

3. Beside each of your commitments listed above, rank yourself on how well to this point in your life you have followed through. Use the 1-10 ranking system, with 1 being not at all and 10 being on the level of Jepthah.

4. How would you have liked the story of Jepthah to end? How might the story have ended if you had been in the place of Jepthah?

5. Why do you think that God is so strict with promises and vows?

Samson
Evil Companions Corrupt
Judges 16

1 One day Samson went to the Philistine town of Gaza and spent the night with a prostitute. 2 Word soon spread that Samson was there, so the men of Gaza gathered together and waited all night at the town gates. They kept quiet during the night, saying to themselves, "When the light of morning comes, we will kill him." 3 But Samson stayed in bed only until midnight. Then he got up, took hold of the doors of the town gate, including the two posts, and lifted them up, bar and all. He put them on his shoulders and carried them all the way to the top of the hill across from Hebron.

4 Some time later Samson fell in love with a woman named Delilah, who lived in the valley of Sorek. 5 The rulers of the Philistines went to her and said, "Entice Samson to tell you what makes him so strong and how he can be overpowered and tied up securely. Then each of us will give you 1,100 pieces of silver." 6 So Delilah said to Samson, "Please tell me what makes you so strong and what it would take to tie you up securely."

7 Samson replied, "If I were tied up with seven new bowstrings that have not yet been dried, I would become as weak as anyone else." 8 So the Philistine rulers brought Delilah seven new bowstrings, and she tied Samson up with them. 9 She had hidden some men in one of the inner rooms of her house, and she cried out, "Samson! The Philistines have come to capture you!" But Samson snapped the bowstrings as a piece of string snaps when it is burned by a fire. So the secret of his strength was not discovered.

10 Afterward Delilah said to him, "You've been making fun of me and telling me lies! Now please tell me how you can be tied up securely." 11 Samson replied, "If I were tied up with brand-new ropes that had never been used, I would become as weak as anyone else." 12 So Delilah took new ropes and tied him up with them. The men were hiding in the inner room as before, and again Delilah cried out, "Samson! The Philistines have come to capture you!" But again Samson snapped the ropes from his arms as if they were thread.

13 Then Delilah said, "You've been making fun of me and telling me lies! Now tell me how you can be tied up securely." Samson replied, "If you were to weave the seven braids of my hair into the fabric on your loom and tighten it with the loom shuttle, I would become as weak as anyone else." So while he slept, Delilah wove the seven braids of his hair into the fabric. 14 Then she tightened it with the loom shuttle. Again she cried out, "Samson! The Philistines have come to capture you!" But Samson woke up, pulled back the loom shuttle, and yanked his hair away from the loom and the fabric.

15 Then Delilah pouted, "How can you tell me, 'I love you,' when you don't share your secrets with me? You've made fun of me three times now, and you still haven't told me what makes you so strong!" 16 She tormented him with her nagging day after day until he was sick to death of it.

17 Finally, Samson shared his secret with her. "My hair has never been cut," he confessed, "for I was dedicated to God as a Nazirite from birth. If my head were shaved, my strength would leave me, and I would become as weak as anyone else."

18 Delilah realized he had finally told her the truth, so she sent for the Philistine rulers. "Come back one more time," she said, "for he has finally told me his secret." So the Philistine rulers returned with the money in their hands. 19 Delilah lulled Samson to sleep with his head in her lap, and then she called in a man to shave off the seven locks of his hair. In this way she began to bring him down, and his strength left him.

20 Then she cried out, "Samson! The Philistines have come to capture you!" When he woke up, he thought, "I will do as before and shake myself free." But he didn't realize the LORD had left him.

21 So the Philistines captured him and gouged out his eyes. They took him to Gaza, where he was bound with bronze chains and forced to grind grain in the prison.

22 But before long, his hair began to grow back.

23 The Philistine rulers held a great festival, offering sacrifices and praising their god, Dagon. They said, "Our god has given us victory over our enemy Samson!" 24 When the people saw him, they praised their god, saying, "Our god has delivered our enemy to us! The one who killed so many of us is now in our power!" 25 Half drunk by now, the people demanded, "Bring out Samson so he can amuse us!" So he was brought from the prison to amuse them, and they had him stand between the pillars supporting the roof.

26 Samson said to the young servant who was leading him by the hand, "Place my hands against the pillars that hold up the temple. I want to rest against them." 27 Now the temple was completely filled with people. All the Philistine rulers were there, and there were about 3,000 men and women on the roof who were watching as Samson amused them.

28 Then Samson prayed to the LORD, "Sovereign LORD, remember me again. O God, please strengthen me just one more time. With one blow let me pay back the Philistines for the loss of my two eyes." 29 Then Samson put his hands on the two center pillars that held up the temple. Pushing against them with both hands, 30 he prayed, "Let me die with the Philistines." And the temple crashed down on the Philistine rulers and all the people. So he killed more people when he died than he had during his entire lifetime.

Sometimes in life, the problems that we experience...or the messes we have to endure....are the direct result of the bad relationships we choose to have. Ever thought about it? Mom may have been right when she told us not to hang around that person that we most likely hung around anyway! Bad friends DO corrupt good morals.

We see this in the life of Samson. You remember him, the gladiator of all gladiators. The muscle guy of all biceps. The babe magnet of the Old Testament. He's usually the guy we as men most idolize and wish we were like. Might need to rethink that one....

God gave Samson a unique gift from his very conception. He had been dedicated to God and was to live as a Nazarite, a special follower of God. He was also to deliver the Israelites from the Philistines and his hair was never to be cut. Remember when we explained earlier about the Spirit of the Lord coming upon men in the Old Testament, allowing them to do great things. Well, that was the case with Samson as well.

Samson had incredible physical strength, but very poor judgment in his relationships with women. He attempted to marry a Philistine woman, but she married his best man. Samson was so angry that he took 300 foxes, tied their tails together, set them on fire and let them run through the Philistine fields, grapevines and olive trees. He certainly put a hot time in that old town that night!

Through a series of other stories, it was discovered that no one could actually tie him up and hold him down. His strength always broke any cords or ropes used on him.

As his tendency toward bad relationships continued, so did his unbridled anger. On one occasion, he sought out a prostitute. When the Philistines tried to capture him, he disappeared, along with the city gates he had run through. I suppose he must have needed them for something, even though it most likely took 20 men to hang them on their hinges in the first place!

The older Samson got, the worse his decisions were about women. Still not learning to leave Philistine women alone, he fell in love with Delilah. The Philistine leaders solicited her help in finding his source or strength…or weakness as the case may be. Through several lies and attempted captures, hope seemed weak that Delilah would ever find out the truth. Then one day, Delilah played the "If you loved me" game. You know this game. Women will pull this card sometimes to see how many hoops we will jump through in order to prove our love for them. She nagged Samson until he could stand it no longer! He revealed his secret to her and when he went to sleep, she had his head shaved, his strength removed and his dignity lost.

The Philistines were able to capture him, gouge out his eyes and take him to grind out grain. One day when they were celebrating a pagan festival, they drunkenly decided to have great entertainment with Samson, humiliating him in public. They brought him to the open area and had him lean against the temple pillars that supported the roof. No one noticed or truly understood that Samson's hair had begun to grow back…along with his sense of righteousness.

While he was leaning against the pillars, he began to pray. Like us today, when we are at the very bottom of the pit, we oftentimes turn to God in need. And like with Samson, God always responds to a broken heart and an appeal for righteousness. The harder Samson prayed, the stronger he became. (Remember that principle next time you start praying!!) God empowered him to be able to push the pillars down, causing the temple to crash and all the people in it to be killed. That is the redeeming part of the story, but the fact is, Samson died in the rubble as well.

God may rescue you physically sometimes, but He will always rescue you spiritually. Yes, it would have been a great story if his eyesight had returned along with his strength. It would have been a happy ending if he died many years later with a wife of many years and children and grandchildren surrounding him, swinging from his Tarzan strength arms. But sometimes we have to suffer the consequences of our behaviors. These consequences remind us of the response required of us from God in remaining righteous. God's patience is strong, but it is not bottomless.

Challenge:
Think this week about the ways God has empowered you to be strong for him. Also, consider the weaknesses that you have that could easily do you in. "MAN UP" this week and admit them.

Discussion Questions

1. What are the strengths you have as a man of God? List them below:

2. What are the weaknesses you have that can ruin your strengths if you don't keep them bridled? Share some of these with the group if you feel comfortable in doing this.

3. Think back on lessons (both positive and negative) you have learned in your relationships with women. Share some of these with the men around you.

Eli
Leading the People, but Losing the Kids
I Samuel 2:12

12 Now the sons of Eli were scoundrels who had no respect for the LORD.

S ometimes, it's easier to do the "Lord's work" or "church work" than it is to work on the family at home. In church work, there is usually an immediate consequence to what is done, making it easier to see the fruits of our labors. We can also leave it at the office and go home if we want to. Working on our marriage, our children, and the family overall is much harder to do. The results of these efforts many times take years to see, if ever. Now, I know that most of you are not preachers or elders (hopefully some of you are!), but working for God is great. But it is no substitute for where we have truly been called to serve...and that is in our own home. So, whether you are filling your time with church work or just work, weigh the long term importance of your efforts. Training your children for the next generation has much more lasting effects...and is much more important!

Eli and his sons seem to be a good example of this principle. Eli was a priest of God (or in those days, a preacher, elder or ministry leader type.) You may recall that Eli was the priest serving at the place of worship when a woman named Hannah came to pray. We get a glimpse of Eli's true core nature when we see him rebuking her for being drunk when he sees her praying with more fervor than he had ever seen. Now, to his credit, she might have been drunk. In the story however, he does not investigate to see if she is indeed in the throes of pain and desperation. He just assumes that she is not right.

Eli had sons who were also priests, and the Bible describes them as "scoundrels"—-true "preacher's kids" in the worst sense of the word! These sons had no respect for the Lord. Instead, they used their God-given position within the tribe of Levi (the priestly tribe in the Old Testament) as a means of entitlement. Basically, they took what they wanted when they wanted it, including the meat from the sacrifices made to God. And they did this with force and intimidation.

They also took what they wanted from the young women working at the entrance of the Tabernacle. Their sins were widely known; and according to the scripture, Eli did plead with them to stop their wicked ways. This seems like he is doing a good parenting thing...and he was. The main problem comes with the understanding of how Eli felt about his sons. God tells us that Eli honored his sons MORE than he honored God. This wasn't just a case of grown children making bad choices...and being responsible entirely for themselves. By allowing his sons to continue in their evil ways, he was showing greater honor to them than to God. From what we can understand about the story, Eli had not himself stolen meat from the sacrifices of the people, but he had eaten it along with his sons...and gotten fat from it just like his sons.

Honoring your children more than honoring God is a very popular philosophy in our world today. Many parents spend more time watching their kids play soccer on Sundays that watching them listen to Bible stories at church. Many parents spend more money on their kids- making them look the best, be the best and get the best- than they would ever consider on giving to missions. Some parents who spend their energy in pushing their kids to succeed and providing opportunities that conflict with spiritual development are living through their children. They didn't have it (the opportunities, the clothes, the new car, etc.) so they want their kids to have it. Some dads feel guilty for spending so much time with their work, they spend the money on their kids to offset the time not spent with them. And some parents don't really think about it much. They may see it as mom's job…or the school's job…or the church's job, to raise their children and give them the morals, character development and life principles they are not giving to them.

Think about where you are with your kids. Are they out of control? Are they spoiled? Are they disrespectful? Ask yourself the question, "What part in this have I played?

To finish the story of Eli, it is NOT a happy ending! Eli was held responsible for his mistakes with his sons and received a message from God that God was tired of it! Not only were both of his sons killed in the same day, but when Eli heard about it, he was overtaken in grief, fell back and killed himself. If that was not bad enough, Eli's family was removed from the priesthood forever and apparently lived a life of poverty for the coming generations.

Talk about the lasting effects of our parenting!

Note: I want to be clear here to say that certainly our children have a mind of their own. They can make their own decisions and are responsible for them once they reach an accountable age. If you do have grown children who have not remained faithful to God or who never did come to a life of faith with Him, that may not be your responsibility. However, we play a major role in the development of our children…and in the development of their faith walk with God. The opportunities we have with our children are precious. For every wasted one we spend either honoring them more than we do God or spending it pursuing other passions of our own, we lose a generation of growth.

-Think of it as preparing your children to parent the next generation.
-Think of the time with them as ways to teach them how to be men and women of God themselves.
-Consider the long term rewards of investing in your children as opposed to investing in wealth or power or personal pleasures.

Hold yourself and your children accountable.

Challenge:
This week, spend time considering a revision of your priority list. Does it need one?

Discussion Questions

1. Evaluate your children's development of faith.
    a. Dependent on their age, are they in love with God and trying to be faithful followers of Him?
    b. How many times do they ask you about religious or spiritual things?
    c. What do you specifically do to aid in their development in this area?
    d. Explore some ideas of how you might be more involved—-things you can provide for them and things you can do with them.

2. Make a list of things that you can do to make things better. Don't allow yourself to leave feeling bad as a father. Empower yourself to do what's better for your children.

Samuel
Listening for God
1 Samuel 3:10

10 And the Lᴏʀᴅ came and called as before, "Samuel! Samuel!" And Samuel replied, "Speak, your servant is listening."

Last week, we discussed the story of Eli, one of the priests of Israel and his very disrespectful and unrighteous sons. We discussed what you might be putting in front of your mate or children and how to better put energy into helping those we love on their faith walk with God. This week, we talk about the one "son" of Eli who turned out right.

Not really his son at all, Samuel was promised back to God if God would grant his mother, Hannah, a child. You remember Hannah. This woman was the one praying so fervently in the temple where Eli was working, that Eli thought she must be drunk. Regardless of the misinterpretation of Eli, God was listening to Hannah and valued her heart. He granted her desire for a son and gave Samuel to her. As promised, Hannah brought Samuel back "to God" after he had grown a bit. Giving him to God meant that she would have to give up her daily relationship with him and let him serve in the daily affairs of priests. Ironically, Hannah knew what it meant to give a child to God whereas Eli did not, since neither of his sons was faithful. Samuel was not only faithful to God, but became one of the leading figures in the Old Testament.

The story that most captures the essence of Samuel was one in his youth. One night when he was going to sleep, he heard a voice calling to him. Thinking that Eli, who had become his caretaker and mentor, was calling h to him, he got up and went to him. After asking him why he had called him, Eli, dismissed the situation and sent him back to bed. Three times this same voice happened. Three times, Samuel went to Eli and asked what he wanted. On the third time, Eli realized that this may be the voice of God. He instructed Samuel to say at the next voice, "Yes, Lord, your servant is listening."

Before continuing with the rest of the story, let's pause to look at some of the contradictions within this Bible occurrence.

1. Eli, once again, shows us that even though we may call ourselves religious (or religious leader) we often times miss the opportunity to hear God and to serve Him. Isn't it sad that Eli continues to show his lack of personal connection with the God he was serving as priest? Eli had questioned the prayers of a fervent follower of God, maybe because he had never prayed to God so fervently himself. He missed the opportunity to train his own sons in the service of God because he valued them more than he did God. And now, it takes 3 times for a young man who has been given over to the service of God to recognize that God might be talking to him. I wonder if God had stopped talking to Eli. I also wonder if Eli had stopped listening to God?

2. God calls a young, inexperienced, good hearted kid, rather than the seasoned professional, to talk to. Never think that you are not good enough, or experienced enough, or religious enough for God to use you. It may be the ones of us whose lives are broken or whose hearts are not shaded by our own greed and worldly concerns that God can most use!

3. Many times we mistake God's voice for coincidence. I was in a state of transition with one of my jobs a long time ago. I did not know which direction to go or how it might affect my young family. In an effort to do the right thing, I wrestled and struggled and worried and then did all those things over again. The thing I didn't do was to pray and listen for

God. Things started happening. Two doors closed and one door remained open. I jumped at it. Looking back on that, it was exactly the right thing to do, but it wasn't my doing of it. God had tried to tell me what to do. I wasn't listening. For several years after the event, I said both publicly and privately how glad I was that this job had "coincidentally" worked out, because it was the best thing for me and my family. I now realize that there was no coincidence to it at all. God had directed my path even when I was not listening! In an effort to be real "men," we will deny our helplessness and confusion and bull our way through a bad situation, crossing our fingers that things will work out.

Now, you might be saying, "Ray, if I really heard a voice from God, you would put me on a drug and put me in therapy." And mostly, that would be true. As we have discussed before in this series, God speaks to us in several different ways-
- through His Word
- through odd or special circumstances
- in the voice of a friend or loved one
- in a deep sense of calm or peace
- and many more!

What I would like to suggest are two things:
1. that somewhere through the process, we give God a chance to speak up. We do that by asking and then listening. We do that by asking for guidance before we make all the decisions and then asking God to "baptize" the answer we want to hear.
2. that somewhere after the process, we give God the credit and glory for what has been done for us and how things did work out so wonderfully. This accomplishes a couple of things. It lets others know that they can do this also- trust in God and wait for Him to lead our lives. It also reinforces in our own minds that God does call us and wants us to listen to Him. God always has our best interest in mind. We oftentimes are only interested in what we have on our mind that interests

us! Many times that is in the present, and not in the long range plans of our lives.

Challenge:
This week focus on listening intently to what God wants you to hear.

Discussion Questions

1. Listening to God is a really difficult discipline to learn. How have you learned it over the years?

2. Have you had experiences in the past that you chalked up to "coincidence" or luck or whatever except God? In what way(s) has God played a role in your past life in which you did not give Him credit?

3. God does not really need the "credit" from what He does, but others need the example and encouragement when they see what God does in other people's lives. Who played a role in letting you see that they listened to God? How did this affect you? How do you share with others that God has a role in leading you?

4. We would hope that "church" would play a positive place in our development as spiritual beings. The story above suggests that it might not always happen that way. Describe to others in the group how you think your past participation in "church" or "church things" helped or hindered your relationship with God.

Saul
Knowing When to Keep Your Mouth Shut
I Sam 10:26-27

26 When Saul returned to his home at Gibeah, a group of men whose hearts God had touched went with him. 27 But there were some scoundrels who complained, "How can this man save us?" And they scorned him and refused to bring him gifts. But Saul ignored them.

You may recognize the name Saul as the first King of Israel. We don't have time to go into that whole process, but know that his only qualifications were that he was really tall and handsome. Well, that's what people want, even nowadays, right?

One day, donkeys belonging to Saul's father strayed away. Saul and one of his servants went looking for them. They traveled all over the territory looking for the donkeys without success. Finally, Saul suggested that they go home. He knew that his father would be concerned about them, and quite frankly how long can you look for lost donkeys?

The servant suggested that they see the prophet of God living in this town as he might be able to tell them where the donkeys were. Upon inquiry, they learned that there was to be a public sacrifice and that they might be able to find Samuel, the Lord's prophet, there. Sure enough, as they headed into town, Samuel was coming out. In fact, he told them that he had been looking for them as the donkeys had been found. He then insisted that they stay with him and be the honored guests at the sacrificial meal. They agreed.

The next morning, Samuel took Saul aside and
- anointed him with oil
- kissed him
- gave specific instructions as to where the donkeys could be found
- AND TOLD HIM THAT HE HAD BEEN CHOSEN BY GOD TO BE ISRAEL'S FIRST KING!

At that moment, the Spirit of the Lord came upon Saul and he began to prophesy while he met a group of prophets. Saul then found the donkeys and went home. When his uncle asked him about the travels and the donkey-search, Saul told him that Samuel had helped him find the donkeys. He did not tell him that Samuel had also anointed him King.

Saul knew that telling the leaders that God had already chosen him to be King would make then angry- either to the point of not making him King or perhaps stoning him. Saul learned a lesson that we all need at one point or another in our lives- KNOWING WHEN TO KEEP YOUR MOUTH SHUT! Now, I am not sure how you might have handled this situation, but I might very well have paraded myself right into the city announcing (or having others announce in front of me), that I was the newly appointed King and that God Himself had told me so! Personal pride will many times prevent us from being both humble and restraining in telling others about our good fortune.

When Samuel met with the tribal leaders before the Lord to select a king, the leaders selected Saul. When they looked for him, they could not find him. The Lord told them that he was hiding in the baggage. This suggests that Saul was not just humble, but a little afraid. I always wished this part of the story was not in there, until I learned that most of us who struggle with humility (or the lack of it) also struggle with confidence. I am sure you have heard of the superiority complex being the cover up for an inferiority complex. The two extremes seem to go hand in hand. Saul may have been very confident in his good looks, but not at all confident in his good leadership. In fact, years later this will become Saul's downfall. Like Saul, we take pride in things that we do well, but overlook or compensate for the areas of our life we are weak in. It might have served Saul well to work in the weak areas instead of compensating for them.

Back to the story…Samuel found Saul and presented him as God's choice. Coming from the voice of a prophet that he had been chosen King was probably better than coming from his own voice! Saul's restraint was a good thing here. Saul later displays the same restraint when God sent a band of men whose hearts were touched to be his constant companions. Not everyone was pleased. While some complained, others began to hate him. Once again Saul kept his mouth shut and refused to go into a rage.

Certainly not for all of Saul's life did he show such restraint. A few years later, God selects David to be the next king of Israel. Saul is so jealous that he tries to kill him several times. Without discipline and true restraint, we all might get to the level of the misbehavior of Saul.

Challenge:
Ask yourself in what areas of your life there is a need for restraint. It might not be in talking or speaking for you, but it may very well be in another area.

Discussion Questions:

1. List 3 top areas of your life in which you need to practice restraint.

   a.

   b.

   c.

2. List things you have tried in the past that did NOT work in these areas.

3. List new ideas you might try in order to restrain yourself.

4. How do you respond when people criticize you?

5. How does keeping quiet help accomplish something?

6. In order to carry out God's mission for your life, who do you keep company with? Who might you need to withdraw from in order to be better? Who is a strong encouragement for you and association should be expanded?

7. Explore the idea of NOT keeping your mouth shut. When might it be in the best interest to open your mouth and use your voice to say something?

David

Focus or Blips
2 Samuel 11:1-17

1 In the spring of the year, when kings normally go out to war, David sent Joab and the Israelite army to fight the Ammonites. They destroyed the Ammonite army and laid siege to the city of Rabbah. However, David stayed behind in Jerusalem.

2 Late one afternoon, after his midday rest, David got out of bed and was walking on the roof of the palace. As he looked out over the city, he noticed a woman of unusual beauty taking a bath. 3 He sent someone to find out who she was, and he was told, "She is Bathsheba, the daughter of Eliam and the wife of Uriah the Hittite." 4 Then David sent messengers to get her; and when she came to the palace, he slept with her. She had just completed the purification rites after having her menstrual period. Then she returned home. 5 Later, when Bathsheba discovered that she was pregnant, she sent David a message, saying, "I'm pregnant."

6 Then David sent word to Joab: "Send me Uriah the Hittite." So Joab sent him to David. 7 When Uriah arrived, David asked him how Joab and the army were getting along and how the war was progressing. 8 Then he told

Uriah, "Go on home and relax" David even sent a gift to Uriah after he had left the palace. 9 But Uriah didn't go home. He slept that night at the palace entrance with the king's palace guard.

10 When David heard that Uriah had not gone home, he summoned him and asked, "What's the matter? Why didn't you go home last night after being away for so long?"

11 Uriah replied, "The Ark and the armies of Israel and Judah are living in tents, and Joab and my master's men are camping in the open fields. How could I go home to wine and dine and sleep with my wife? I swear that I would never do such a thing."

12 "Well, stay here today," David told him, "and tomorrow you may return to the army." So Uriah stayed in Jerusalem that day and the next. 13 Then David invited him to dinner and got him drunk. But even then he couldn't get Uriah to go home to his wife. Again he slept at the palace entrance with the king's palace guard.

14 So the next morning David wrote a letter to Joab and gave it to Uriah to deliver. 15 The letter instructed Joab, "Station Uriah on the front lines where the battle is fiercest. Then pull back so that he will be killed." 16 So Joab assigned Uriah to a spot close to the city wall where he knew the enemy's strongest men were fighting. 17 And when the enemy soldiers came out of the city to fight, Uriah the Hittite was killed along with several other Israelite soldiers.

There are many things each day that "blip" across our visual field like blips on a radar screen. It's what we choose to FOCUS on that speaks volumes about out character. That "focused blip" has the ability to modify the rest of our choices and impact our future lives.

Such is the case with David and his visual blips. Instead of being with his troops in the war zone as they fought the Ammonites, David stayed in Jerusalem and entrusted the battle to others. Instead of going to war, David took a nap, followed by a walk up on the roof—-a vantage point for viewing the city and its activities. One of the blips on David's radar screen that afternoon was Bathsheba, the wife of Uriah the Hittite. Uriah was one of David's mighty men! But instead of letting Bathsheba "blip" across the screen, David decided to focus on her. The rest of his life became altered accordingly.

Not only did David focus on Bathsheba as she bathed, but he sent his servants to find out who she was. I wonder if his servants got a glimpse that David was focusing in the wrong direction, that he might be going down a path he shouldn't be taking? I also wonder why they did not tell him. After all, David is referred to as "a man after God's own heart." Wouldn't he surround himself by trusted and trustworthy people? Wouldn't they feel some compulsion to warn him or at least question him? Perhaps they knew he wouldn't listen to them, as they were lowly servants. We might all learn to listen to the counsel of all around us. Everyone has something to share with us on our life's journey.

Upon finding out that she was married to one of his trusted warriors, he implemented a plan to get her husband out of the way. As the seduction process continued, Bathsheba became pregnant and David attempted to get Uriah to sleep with his own wife. This would allow David to claim that the child was really his. But that just didn't happen. Uriah was so focused on his commitment as a warrior of David's, that he would not leave his troops or his king and enjoy the pleasures of home if his troops could not. David's plan was thwarted.

When all else failed, David devised a plan to have Uriah killed in battle. He had one of his commanders put Uriah in the front of the men and then withdraw the other men so that Uriah would be killed in battle. Unfortunately, this plan worked for David. Bathsheba mourned for her husband for the appropriate time. When her mourning was done, David moved her to the palace, and she became one of his wives.

Their son was soon born, but the consequences of our sins usually always follow us. Their child died because God was not at all pleased with David's behaviors.

Just like David, so much of our lives are influenced and shaped by the things upon which we choose to focus. It is even easy to lose the big picture of right and wrong when we get so focused on the sins and temptations of our lives.

Being distracted by a blip on the radar screen is no big deal. It happens hundreds of times a day. We have the options to stay distracted many times and choose not to do so. Then comes that one temptation that we cannot seem to shake. We just can't get it out of our minds. It just won't let us go. Or so we think. It is never the temptation that will not let US go, it is US who will not let the temptation go.

Stopping long enough to focus is a dangerous thing for any of us. Losing focus and forgetting about the big picture is potentially life threatening...at least out spiritual life!

Think for a minute about the things on your radar screen that cause you the most trouble. We've talked in this series about these kinds of temptations already. Now it is time to face them and put in precautions for future problems.

Is it:
Sexual issues?
Money and greed?
Power and control?
An addictive substance?
A prescription drug?
An old flame?

Challenge:
This week spend time being more aware of the blips that come across your screen that are good. How might you act upon those?

Discussion Questions

1. In the space below, list the 3 top things you have had the opportunity to change from a blip into a focus. How did you handle it?

2. How might you be able to avoid that temptation in the future?

3. What else might you spend your time doing in order to not be "available" for these sins?

Solomon
Head and Heart- God Wants Both
I Kings 4:29-30

29 God gave Solomon very great wisdom and understanding, and knowledge as vast as the sands of the seashore. 30 In fact, his wisdom exceeded that of all the wise men of the East and the wise men of Egypt.

Solomon was David's son and became King following David's reign. Solomon was feeling overwhelmed by the responsibility of governing a nation of people that were too many to be counted. So, when God appeared to him in a dream and told him to ask for anything he wanted, Solomon asked for an understanding mind and the ability to know the difference between right and wrong. Solomon acknowledged that there was no way he could govern this nation well without God's help.

Pause here with me and think…

Wouldn't it be awesome if we felt the same way about our families, our churches, and our lives? We are raised as men to feel that we should be in control and be able to handle anything. Asking for help and admitting our weaknesses is not very "manly." I wonder if our view of needing God to make good decisions is a sign of weakness…..or a sign of strength?

Anyway, God was pleased with Solomon's realization about his own need. Because Solomon asked God for wisdom and understanding rather than wealth and fame spoke volumes to God about his heart. Because Solomon had his heart and his priorities in the right place, God told him that he would receive what he asked for...and what he hadn't asked for! Solomon's reign as king would surpass and exceed all other kings. In addition to all this, he was promised long life if he followed God's commands obediently.

As you can see in the scripture reading above, God did indeed keep His promise regarding Solomon's wisdom. His knowledge and understanding were immeasurable and far exceeded that of any other king. His wealth was unsurpassed, and his knowledge on all issues and topics was so great that kings sent their ambassadors to him just to listen to his wisdom.

It sounds like a great story, and it is. But as you can imagine, as time went on, things changed. Solomon's initial response before God- that wisdom was his first priority and that riches were secondary- began to change. By I Kings 10:23, the riches are listed first and the wisdom is second. Even though this may seem subtle in the scriptures, we watch Solomon take his first commitment off God and begin to put it on his desires for himself.

At that point, Solomon began to marry foreign women, and they began to turn his head toward foreign gods. God had already expressly forbidden this. What God said would happen if people began to marry foreign people began to happen to Solomon. He started worshipping false gods. Eventually, Solomon began doing evil in God's sight, made God angry and would not listen to God's commands.

What in the world was Solomon thinking? To be such a smart guy, he certainly became awfully stupid!

As we imagine what in the world would have caused Solomon to turn his head and his heart away from God, we are amazed that that he is worshipping idols made of rock and stone who had nothing to give to him as God had given things to him. And he certainly knows better...So... What could possibly have happened?

Could it be the same things that cause US to turn away from the God from whom all blessing flow? Do we also turn to false idols of worshipping jobs, money, cars, jewelry or even children? Think about it. No matter how much wisdom or knowledge we have, it won't hold us true to God's Word without our heart commitment being aligned as well.

I realize that it is difficult for men to get their heart around caring about spiritual things....church things.....family things.

During this series of studies, we have already looked at the things that tempt us, the things that distract us or cause us to turn blips into a focus. This week let's concentrate on the things that make our hearts happy and that make us realize the beauty of following God.

Challenge:
This week focus on the wisdom that comes from God, as it differs from worldly wisdom.

Discussion Questions

1. What particular area of life do you need wisdom in? What methods do you use to acquire it? How does that work for you?

2. Wisdom may be the putting of knowledge to "practical use in an effective and right way." How would your life be different if you had more practical wisdom?

3. What part(s) of worship work for you? (i.e. make sense and help you grow spiritually)

4. What makes sense to you about following God?

5. What about God, religion or spirituality do you find makes little or no sense to you? Share this with the group and try to understand what others struggle with MORE than trying within your group to answer each others' questions.

6. As men, are we hardwired to take too much pride in our talents, whatever they may be? How could Solomon have remained more humble? How can you remain more humble?

7. It appears that even being the smartest man ever did not prevent Solomon from sinning. What does that tell you about mankind and our need for forgiveness?

Azariah
Sticking with God
II Chronicles 15:1-2

1 Then the Spirit of God came upon Azariah son of Oded, 2 and he went out to meet King Asa as he was returning from the battle. "Listen to me, Asa!" he shouted. "Listen, all you people of Judah and Benjamin! The LORD will stay with you as long as you stay with him! Whenever you seek him, you will find him. But if you abandon him, he will abandon you.

Later in the Israelites' history, their kingdom divides. Asa is one of the few good kings of Judah during this time. He attempted to do what was pleasing in God's sight by ridding the nation of all the false gods, Asherah poles, incense burners, and pagan altars and shrines. He led the people in seeking the Lord, the Jehovah God of their ancestors. He encouraged them to serve Him ONLY! The result of this was that God gave Asa and his kingdom a time of peace and rest. For ten years, God allowed Asa's people the opportunity to build up the kingdom. They built up the fortified cities with walls, towers and gates. More importantly, they gave God all the glory for this by proclaiming to all the people around them that God, the Jehovah God had provided for them this rest.

King Asa was also able to build up the armies of two of the tribes of Israel, Judah and Benjamin. In fact, when a million-man army from Ethiopia attacked them, Asa was able to pray to God as he deployed his vast army…and God gave them a victory! Now you might be thinking to this point in the story, "Why aren't you talking about Asa in this chapter?" We certainly could do that. Asa stood up against the people who were doing wrong. He had done what was right more than what was popular. He had put God at the forefront and made everyone see the glory of God. He truly was a mighty man himself! But this story continues with even a better lesson for us this week.

When Asa returned home from battle, the Prophet Azariah went to meet him. Prophets were selected men who spoke on behalf of God (that's what "to prophecy" means) and in most cases had to confront a really bad situation in order to speak for God. Some of them yelled. Others behaved very peculiarly to get their message across. Most threatened doom and destruction just to get people's attention…not to mention if the correct response was not followed!

Azariah was different. He was filled with the Spirit of God. He simply, but boldly exclaimed to the people that as long as they chose to remain with God, He would remain with them. But, if the people chose to abandon God and return to idolatry, God would abandon them. He reminded them of how He had always been there to care for the people as long as they stayed with Him. He encouraged the people to be strong and courageous in their devotion. That's it. That's as bad and "doom-ful" as it gets.

Encouraged by Azariah's message, the people continued to get rid of all the idolatry. They then offered sacrifices to God and entered into a covenant (a binding promise) to seek the Lord God with all their heart and soul.

So, why would Azariah be picked over Asa as an example of a mighty man this week? Here's the deal:

I am not sure how many of you were raised on guilt and condemnation, particularly within the confines of church or religion, but I was. It is important within this lesson to recognize the effects of an encouraging message. Azariah was one of the few prophets who delivered his message in a positive, encouraging and uplifting way. It was simple, to the point and non-threatening. It was certainly being supported in the story by the actions of Asa, but its simple message was remarkable.

I wonder if a more positive response might come more often nowadays from a more positive message about the grace of Jesus or the love of God. Certainly, we can swing to one extreme at the exclusion of the other. A strong balance is needed to be fair with God and His message...but wouldn't it be nice to hear some good things every now and then?

As we review the lessons in this series, most of them have been pretty hard and confrontational. Perhaps that is good. But this week, I wanted to be sure to encourage you to keep at it. The same message is true for you today as it was for the people of Israel back then. God will bless and keep you...if you continue to seek Him.

If you don't...well, start over with chapter one of this series. The judgment of the Lord may be upon you.

Challenge:
This week, concentrate on "remaining in the Lord" and on the blessings God has already given you.

Discussion Questions

1. What do you think is meant by the phrase, "remain in the Lord?"

2. How do you evaluate if God is "with you?"

3. How might remaining in the Lord on a daily basis modify your daily life?

4. Take a fair look at your religious upbringing. Was there negativism in the messages you heard? Was grace talked about? What about forgiveness? Did others tell you that seeing God as a positive and loving God was too soft?

5. How do you view God now? Hard or soft? Gentle or vengeful? Firm or forgiving? As you think about these and share your ideas with others in the group, know that God is BOTH...an appropriate balance of both extremes.

6. How do you measure up to being and exhibiting a strong and healthy balance of these sides of God with others around you?

Josiah
What are you worshipping?
II Chronicles 34: 1-33

Josiah was eight years old when he became king, and he reigned in Jerusalem thirty-one years. 2 He did what was pleasing in the LORD's sight and followed the example of his ancestor David. He did not turn away from doing what was right.

3 During the eighth year of his reign, while he was still young, Josiah began to seek the God of his ancestor David. Then in the twelfth year he began to purify Judah and Jerusalem, destroying all the pagan shrines, the Asherah poles, and the carved idols and cast images. 4 He ordered that the altars of Baal be demolished and that the incense altars which stood above them be broken down. He also made sure that the Asherah poles, the carved idols, and the cast images were smashed and scattered over the graves of those who had sacrificed to them. 5 He burned the bones of the pagan priests on their own altars, and so he purified Judah and Jerusalem.

8 In the eighteenth year of his reign, after he had purified the land and the Temple, Josiah appointed Shaphan son of Azaliah, Maaseiah the governor of Jerusalem, and Joah son of Joahaz, the royal historian, to repair the Temple of the LORD his God. 9 They gave Hilkiah the high priest the money that had been collected by the Levites who served as gatekeepers at the Temple of God. The gifts were brought by people from Manasseh, Ephraim, and from all the remnant of Israel, as well as from all Judah, Benjamin, and the people of Jerusalem.

10 He entrusted the money to the men assigned to supervise the restoration of the LORD's Temple. Then they paid the workers who did the repairs and renovation of the Temple. 11 They hired carpenters and builders, who purchased finished stone for the walls and timber for the rafters and beams. They restored what earlier kings of Judah had allowed to fall into ruin.

14 While they were bringing out the money collected at the LORD's Temple, Hilkiah the priest found the Book of the Law of the LORD that was written by Moses. 15 Hilkiah said to Shaphan the court secretary, "I have found the Book of the Law in the LORD's Temple!"

19 When the king heard what was written in the Law, he tore his clothes in despair. 20 Then he gave these orders to Hilkiah, Ahikam son of Shaphan, Acbor son of Micaiah, Shaphan the court secretary, and Asaiah the king's personal adviser: 21 "Go to the Temple and speak to the LORD for me and for all the remnant of Israel and Judah. Inquire about the words written in the scroll that has been found. For the LORD's great anger has been poured out on us because our ancestors have not obeyed the word of the LORD. We have not been doing everything this scroll says we must do."

22 So Hilkiah and the other men went to the New Quarter of Jerusalem to consult with the prophet Huldah. 23 She said to them, "The LORD, the God of Israel, has spoken! Go back and tell the man who sent you, 24 'This is what the LORD says: I am going to bring disaster on this city and its people. All the curses written in the scroll that was read to the king of Judah will come true. 25 For my people have abandoned me and offered sacrifices to pagan gods, and I am very angry with them for everything they have done. My anger will be poured out on this place, and it will not be quenched.'

26 "But go to the king of Judah who sent you to seek the Lord and tell him: 'This is what the Lord, the God of Israel, says concerning the message you have just heard: 27 You were sorry and humbled yourself before God when you heard his words against this city and its people. You humbled yourself and tore your clothing in despair and wept before me in repentance. And I have indeed heard you, says the Lord. 28 So I will not send the promised disaster until after you have died and been buried in peace. You yourself will not see the disaster I am going to bring on this city and its people.'" So they took her message back to the king.

29 Then the king summoned all the elders of Judah and Jerusalem. 30 And the king went up to the Temple of the Lord with all the people of Judah and Jerusalem, along with the priests and the Levites—all the people from the greatest to the least. There the king read to them the entire Book of the Covenant that had been found in the Lord's Temple. 31 The king took his place of authority beside the pillar and renewed the covenant in the Lord's presence. He pledged to obey the Lord by keeping all his commands, laws, and decrees with all his heart and soul. He promised to obey all the terms of the covenant that were written in the scroll. 32 And he required everyone in Jerusalem and the people of Benjamin to make a similar pledge. The people of Jerusalem did so, renewing their covenant with God, the God of their ancestors.

33 So Josiah removed all detestable idols from the entire land of Israel and required everyone to worship the LORD their God. And throughout the rest of his lifetime, they did not turn away from the LORD, the God of their ancestors.

Of all the kings of Israel in the Old Testament, Josiah was the youngest ever. He became king at the tender age of 8 years of age. During his time period, idolatry was rampant. Josiah's reign followed an abundance of evil kings who neither sought God for themselves nor imposed the worship of Him on the people. It was a time when there were more idols, altars to false gods and Asherah poles (similar to totem poles) than there were crops in the land.

Josiah's great grandfather was Hezekiah. While Josiah's father and grandfather were evil, somehow the seed of God's Word had been passed into his fertile heart. At age 16, he began to seek God. At the age of 20, he began to purge and clean the kingdom. He had all the totems, idols, altars, shrines and images smashed into dust and sprinkled over the graves of those who sacrificed to them. He even burned the bones of all the pagan priests on the altars of their false gods.

Josiah also began the systematic cleaning and restoration of God's temple in Jerusalem. The money collected by the Levites was used to pay workmen to restore the temple. In the process, the written Law that God had given through Moses was found. When Josiah read it, he tore his clothes in grief realizing how far his people had moved away from God's Word...and obeying it.

Think about it for a minute....what young man would care so much about spiritual things? And you might want to consider where you were when you were 16 or 20. Wonder how closely aligned with Josiah you were when you were his age? How spiritually minded? How willing to take a stand and to be an example?

Josiah sent word to Huldah, the prophetess. She responded, saying that all the destruction would be carried out on the people because of their disobedience and total disregard of God's Word. The destruction would come, but because of the faithfulness of Josiah, the destruction would not happen until after his death.

Josiah prepared the nation to celebrate Passover and once again consecrate the people to God. Josiah called all the people together and from the Lord's temple, he read to them the entire book of the Covenant that had been found in the temple. He wanted everyone to know without a doubt what the Lord required of them.

43 "When an evil spirit leaves a person, it goes into the desert, seeking rest but finding none. 44 Then it says, 'I will return to the person I came from.' So it returns and finds its former home empty, swept, and in order. 45 Then the spirit finds seven other spirits more evil than itself, and they all enter the person and live there. And so that person is worse off than before. That will be the experience of this evil generation."

In Matthew 12:43-45, we see Jesus speaking about an evil spirit leaving a person, and the heart being swept empty and clean. But if the heart remains empty, the evil spirit returns with seven other spirits and re-occupy the clean, empty space.

The same thing is true here for Josiah's people. Had he not sought to fill their hearts and minds with God's Word and laws, the evil spirit of idolatry would certainly re-fill their minds. At this point, Josiah was very wise in attempting to fill their hearts and minds with commitment to God and to purge their idolatrous desires from them.

And this young man is not done in the story yet!

As Josiah attempted to spur the hearts of the people to a consecrated relationship with God, he also organized and established once again the celebration of the Passover. You might recall that just before the Jews were led out of the land of Egypt, where they had been abused slaves, they were instructed in a special behavior to put lamb's blood over their door frames. The angel "passed over" these homes, leaving the families intact. If a family did not have the blood over the doorpost, the first born of the family was killed. Ever since that time, the Jews have celebrated the "Passover", remembering when the Lord protected them from death. Of course, we know now from the New Testament, that this feast (The Passover) was the feast Jesus was celebrating with His apostles when He instituted what we now know as the Lord's Supper or Communion. It has always been, and still is, an awesome celebration in which God unites Himself with His people spiritually.

Now you understand why failure to celebrate the Passover, with all it's significance, was a major breaking away of the people from God. Josiah was right in reinstituting this celebration and trying to refocus the people's attention back to God. When he held this Passover feast, it was a monumental feast. Chapter 35:17-18 says that the people celebrated the Passover and Festival of Unleavened Bread for 7 days. Never, since the days of the prophet Samuel, had there been such a Passover celebration. No other king ever kept Passover as Josiah did!

17 All the Israelites present in Jerusalem celebrated Passover and the Festival of Unleavened Bread for seven days. 18 Never since the time of the prophet Samuel had there been such a Passover. None of the kings of Israel had ever kept a Passover as Josiah did, involving all the priests and Levites, all the people of Jerusalem, and people from all over Judah and Israel.

What an inspiring view of a young man who had developed spiritually over the years of his life! What an example for us and our sons in becoming God's men! What a lesson- filling bad sides of ourselves with positive God-thoughts!

Challenge:
Evaluate your life and the ways you have spiritually developed over the years.
This week, focus on how you perceive your spiritual growth path to be heading. Where might you need to change direction?

Discussion Questions

How did God call you in your youth? Do you remember
how you answered His call?

1. Evaluate the two paths- your faith as a youth and your faith
   as an adult. Do you think you were closer to God then or
   now? Why or why not?

2. Make a list of how you have changed your faith practices
   over the years.

3. What kind of spiritual witness are you giving by your life
   now?

4. If someone knew your faith-walk while growing up, would
   they be impressed with your spiritual development? What
   things would they see?
   * Lessons learned
   * People who influenced you
   * Perceptions held
   * Mistakes made
   * Prayer development
   * Others?

Summary Lesson

This series of "Becoming a MIGHTY MAN of God" has concentrated specifically on overcoming the failures in our lives. We all struggle with issues, with weaknesses, and with the resistance to continue on our path toward God. We have looked at God's men-men who did it right and men who did it terribly wrong. Somewhere in the middle, we may have found our own life example. I am not sure which lesson or group of lessons has spoken most to you throughout this series, but let's take a quick review of the major points of each Mighty Man we studied.

Adam- Being the head of his household was not Adam's strong point. Eve sinned and then enticed her husband to do the same. In what ways did you grow as the head of your household from this lesson? Remember here that the "head of the household" means the person who makes sure things work, and work for the good. You don't get every decision and you don't have to lord it over the members of your home. You do have to assume responsibility for helping every single person in your household find their way and the encouragement to pursue it toward God.

Cain- As our example of anger, Cain taught us that if we don't harness our anger and rage, it will take us out of control. Few of us have probably been convicted of a murder, but we have all destroyed a mood, weakened someone's confidence, or discouraged someone's drive to be better. What anger steps have you taken? Remember, you were just encouraged to do SOMETHING about your anger. How did you do?

Noah- When you read about Noah and realize that he had never even seen rain, much less a boat, it gives us a better sense of the faith it must have taken for him to obey God. Even when it doesn't make sense to us, we need to do what God tells us to do. Remember how Noah must have endured ridicule from the people who watched him! How good are you at obeying God even in the face of being laughed at by your friends or coworkers? Just be thankful, he doesn't ask you to build an ark...

Abraham- What faith it must have taken for Abraham to jump at the voice of God, to be willing to risk everything and follow Him, and to blindly follow the voice of God into a territory where you can only depend on Him. Listen for His voice today- through the Bible, through signs, through other people or through special circumstances. Just listen...and then follow His lead. How have you been doing with that? That blind faith? That open willingness to trust His lead?

Lot- Making decisions for yourself? Lot taught us that we can be selfish if we want to. It never really leads us anywhere, but too many of us struggle with selfishness. How about you?

Isaac- You may not even be married yet, and I'm not sure how close to home this lesson hit you. But if you want to have a close marriage, you have to leave the family you have in a healthy way before that can happen. Being too dependent or being too resentful will prevent this from happening. How are you doing on leaving and then cleaving?

Jacob- We learned the Three Steps to Doom with Jacob. Be careful not to try and run from your problems or your failures. Face them, take the heat and move on. What goes around, comes around. It is better to learn from our mistakes that to ignore them. Got it?

Esau- You have a problem with being the tough guy? The guy who likes to be alone, never sharing his problems and thinking you can make it on your own? Esau taught us that it is never good to be alone. Build close relationships, value what is right and share a little of yourself with those around you. People need people.

Onan- A strange story, remember? Doing what God tells us to do sometimes requires us to do something we really don't want to do. Not only should we do it...but we should want to do it. Onan took the positive side of a responsibility without taking the negative side. How have you done at accepting responsibility for what God wants you to do?

Joseph- Joseph taught us that God really is in control. We can waste our time blaming others for our situations in life, or we can learn from them and give God the glory for where He takes us. We cannot always see the big picture of how God might be using us for His glory, but trust that He will take care of us along the way.

Moses- Has God called you to His service and you just handed Him excuses? Moses beat you to the punch but taught us that in the end, we need to either listen to the Voice or jump in the burning bush. Excuses won't help us grow or help God accomplish His purposes in our world today. Man up!

Pharaoh- How have you learned from Pharaoh's lesson for us? Be careful what you start with God. God may finish it His way. Has your heart been softened toward Him? Have you been humbled? A hard heart won't take you anywhere but to a hard place with God!

Gideon- Lack the faith to do what God tells you to do? Need a little sign to prove that He is real? Gideon showed us that God is patient when we are truly seeking Him. Go ahead. Ask God to show you, convince you, be active in your life. With the right heart and the proper attitude, God may send you a sign. Oh, by the way, God is patient with you too. But, don't make God wait forever!

Jephthah- Jephthah taught us the hard way to be careful bargaining with God and making promises we don't want to keep! God is serious about our commitments- to others and especially to Him. He is faithful and true to His word. How about you? Have you been faithful and true to yours?

Samson- Our true man's man, Samson was a he- man with a she- weakness. In many ways, we all are. Be careful that God is always first in your commitments. Letting your loins do the thinking instead of your brain may cause you to end up in the same mess as Samson...underneath a big old pile of mess you made for yourself!

Eli- Balancing work and family is difficult for all of us. How have you balanced the two? Eli may have worked for God, but he forgot to bring God home with him. How are you doing raising the kids and bringing God home with you? Valuing your children more than you value God is a quick recipe for disaster...just ask Eli.

Samuel- Hearing God speak to you and then being willing to follow Him is a challenge. Samuel showed us that God may have a special plan with you. In all the noise of the world, listen to God's voice calling you to some great service. Have you heard Him yet?

Saul- A lesson we all need to know is how to keep our mouth shut. Knowing when to talk and when to listen is difficult. Saul could have opened his mouth and ruined everything. How are you at knowing when to speak and when to listen?

David- It's not just about sex. There are a hundred different temptations that come across our radar screen every day. The question is: Do we let them stay as blips or do we focus on them? David showed us an example of letting one blip become a passion, and then become a focus, and then an obsession. Be careful not to focus on the wrong things.

Solomon- Solomon taught us that God wants both the head and the heart. One is not enough without the other. As you have thought about that, how are you doing at making God both something to think about and something to cherish. Are you lopsided in your understanding of Him? How should you better balance it?

Azariah- We may have been taught guilt growing up about God and religion, but Azariah showed us that the simple truth can be encouraging and pleasant. You stick with God and He will stick with you. If you were raised in a guilt-ridden religion, know that God's message is not always damnation and doom. His love is awesome and His calling is compassionate.

Josiah- The youngest mighty man in our series, Josiah started reigning as king at age 8 and started doing what God wanted him to do at age 16. You are never too young or too old to begin to do God's will. The point is to grow and mature in the faith. How are you doing with deciding what you will worship in your life? Are you making progress? How will you continue to use this series to grow your faith even deeper?

Well, there you have it....examples of how to become a Mighty Man for God yourself. Take the lessons that speak to you and remind yourself of them regularly. Challenge yourself by remaining close to God and to other men who are challenging themselves too.

The church needs some Mighty Men. Today's church could use examples of listening to God, following Him and growing deeper in their faith along the way. Where will you go from here? Listen for God to tell you. He may be calling you today to learn something, to do something or to be something you could never be on your own.

That's what a Mighty Man is....God's warrior, someone who will fight for what is right and try to be what is right.

That's what He's calling you to be.

Discussion Question

How has this series and God's blessings through it helped you become more of a true Man of God?